Return to Me

Visits to the Tabernacle

Lynda Rozell

Foreword by George Weigel

En Route Books and Media, LLC
Saint Louis, MO

⊛ENROUTE
Make the time

En Route Books and Media, LLC
5705 Rhodes Avenue
St. Louis, MO 63109

Cover credit: Lynda Rozell, photographer, Blessed Sacrament Chapel, Cathedral of St. Matthew the Apostle, Washington, DC. Used with permission.

Copyright © 2024 Lynda Rozell
ISBN-13: 979-8-88870-187-4 and 979-8-88870-203-1
Library of Congress Control Number: 2024938169

Scripture citations from the New American Bible Revised Edition, used within acceptable usage rights as stated at https://www.usccb.org/offices/new-american-bible/permissions. No part of this book may be reproduced, stored in a retrieval system, or transmitted in any form, or by any means, electronic, mechanical, photocopying, or otherwise, without the prior written permission of the author.

Nihil Obstat: + Michael F. Burbidge
Censor Deputatus
Imprimatur: + Michael F. Burbidge
Bishop of Arlington
December 5, 2024

The *nihil obstat* and *imprimatur* are an official declaration that a book, pamphlet, or prayer is free of doctrinal or moral error. No implication is contained therein that those who have granted the *nihil obstat* agree with the contents, opinions, or statements expressed.

DEDICATION

This book is dedicated to the parishioners, staff, and pastor at Our Lady of Perpetual Help in Windham, Maine. As my temporary "home" church, the community welcomed me with kindness and fellowship each day after morning Mass. Father Lou graciously allowed me to use office space with good access to the internet, making it possible to research and write most of this book during my stay in Maine.

ACKNOWLEDGMENTS

I am grateful to the many priests, church representatives, organizations, and artists who gave me permission to use photographs and quotations in this book or directed me to lovely tabernacles I might not otherwise have visited. A few individuals offered to read and comment on the entire manuscript, and others offered additional information about the interpretations of tabernacle art.

I especially thank my amazing beta readers for their comments and editing suggestions: Coleen MacKay, Karen Cassidy, Colin O'Brien, Laura Ruberto, Father Jerry Wooton, Father Lou Phillips, Kathleen March, Joan and George Weigel, and Brian Finnerty.

Bishop Andrew Cozzens, Rose Folsom, Vanessa Denha Garmo, Ever Johnson, and Father Edward Hathaway kindly read and provided pre-publication reviews, despite the many other demands on their time. George Weigel generously wrote the foreword for this work. Thanks to him and his wife, Joan, for their encouragement and friendship.

I am grateful to the Catholic Writers Guild for fellowship and education. A special thanks to my publisher, Dr. Sebastian Mahfood, OP, of En Route Books and Media, LLC, whose enthusiasm and support for this book made it possible to reach a broader audience in record speed.

Finally, I greatly appreciate all the prayers and support of friends and family, both living and on the other side of eternity. All glory and praise to God!

TABLE OF CONTENTS

Foreword by George Weigel iii

Prologue vii

Part One: Introduction 1

    Chapter One: Wonder and Awe 3
    Chapter Two: History and Development of the Tabernacle 13
    Chapter Three: Where to Find Tabernacles 27

Part Two: At The Tabernacle 33

    Chapter Four: Nourishment 35
    Chapter Five: Sacrifice 61
    Chapter Six: Jesus 77
    Chapter Seven: Spirit 115
    Chapter Eight: The Church 129
    Chapter Nine: Mission 145

Part Three: Conclusion 165

    Chapter Ten: Where Our Hearts Find Rest 167

References 173

Appendix: Photographs by State or Other Location 183

FOREWORD

George Weigel

Pope St. John Paul II, whom I had the privilege of knowing for a decade and a half, would have been fascinated by Lynda Rozell. And from his present position in the Communion of Saints, I'm sure he sees in Lynda and her work one fulfillment of his vision for the Catholicism of the twenty-first century and the third millennium.

Throughout his pontificate, and especially during his historic visit to the Holy Land in March 2000, John Paul reminded the Church that the Christian life is a pilgrimage; Lynda's book, *Journeys with a Tin Can Pilgrim*, explains how a recovering lawyer became a pilgrim in service to the evangelizing mission of the Church.

During his years as a priest and bishop in Kraków, Karol Wojtyła was an avid outdoorsman whose summer vacations were spent on kayaking and camping trips with his lay friends; *Tin Can Pilgrim* describes Lynda's ongoing, missionary pilgrimage through camping sites and RV parks.

The "New Evangelization" was the great theme of the second half of John Paul's epic pontificate – a call to Catholics to understand that each of us is baptized into a missionary vocation and that everywhere is mission territory; Lynda Rozell has lived the New Evangelization in a unique way, bringing the Gospel to perhaps unexpecting people in certainly unexpected places – and doing so with a grace, compassion, and fervor that mirrors that of the Polish pope.

And in his last encyclical, *Ecclesia de Eucharistia* [The Church from the Eucharist], John Paul II sought to deepen the Church's faith in the real presence of its eucharistic Lord, not least through the renewal of eucharistic adoration; in this moving book, Lynda takes her readers on a pilgrimage of eucharistic devotion and prayer, centered on the tabernacle – the home of the eucharistic Lord, this side of his return in glory.

Pope St. John Paul II would have loved it.

So would his distinguished successor, Pope Benedict XVI.

As some tabernacles that feature winged angels suggest, the tabernacle in a Catholic Church is the Christian analogue to the Ark of the Covenant – not the magic box of Stephen Spielberg's somewhat blasphemous imagination in *Raiders of the Lost Ark*, but rather the "mercy seat," the repository of the Decalogue, the Ten Commandments given by God to Moses on Mt. Sinai, the design and construction of which are described in Exodus 37:1-9. The Ark was kept in the Holy of Holies, the inner sanctum of the Temple in Jerusalem, which the High Priest could enter only once a year, on Yom Kippur, the Day of Atonement.

In *Jesus of Nazareth – Holy Week: From the Entrance into Jerusalem to the Resurrection,* Pope Benedict suggested that the Ark's role in the rituals of the Day of Atonement helps us grasp who Jesus understood himself to be, and how the first generation of Christians came to understand that this unexpected messiah – a suffering servant rather than a conquering king – fulfilled Israel's hope for a redeemer who would make all things new.

Benedict notes that when St. Paul, in Romans 3:25, wrote about the blood of Christ as an "expiation" for the sins of all, the Apostle to the Gentiles used the Greek equivalent of a Hebrew word for "the covering of the Ark of the Covenant." This, the pope continued, "is the place over which YHWH appears in a cloud, the place of the mysterious presence of God." And it was there, on Yom Kippur, that the blood of the sacrifice of atonement was sprinkled, to expiate the sins of the people over the past year.

Thus, when St. Paul used the equivalent word to explain to the Roman Christians – a congregation of Jewish origin likely centered in the now-funky neighborhood of Trastevere – what has happened through the Christ's self-sacrifice on the Cross, he was teaching them that Israel's God is present to the world in Jesus in a new, radical way: that Jesus understood himself to be the presence of the God of Israel among the people of Israel and in the world. "In him," Pope Benedict wrote, "God and man, God and the world, touch one another..."

As the first Christians gradually came to understand, the Law encoded in the Ten Commandments and the Holy of Holies of the Temple were no longer the exclusive places where God dwelt among his people. Law and Temple had been fulfilled in Jesus, who as Son of God completed the process of God's self-revelation that began with Abraham, Isaac, Jacob, and Moses. As the new Ark of the Covenant, Jesus contains and fulfills all that is precious in the Law ("Think not that I have come to abolish the law and the prophets; I have come not to abolish them but to fulfill them" [Matthew 5:17]). As the sacrificial "Lamb of God, who takes away the sins of the world" [John 1:29], and from whose pierced side blood and water flow forth, giving birth to the Church [John 19:34], Jesus embodies all that was worthy in the Temple cult of sacrifice: its acknowledgment of our dependence on God's mercy for the forgiveness of our sins and the renovation of our spiritual lives.

And so, Pope Benedict concludes, the blood of the New Covenant "which is poured out for many" [Matthew 26:29], brings both Law and Temple to fulfillment, in the forgiveness or expiation of sins that opens the pathway to life in the Kingdom of God among us – a kingdom now present, above all in the Holy Eucharist. Those who become friends of Jesus thereby enter a new world of "transformation and expiation," the experience of which is most profound when we follow the Lord's eucharistic commands, "Take, eat, this is my Body…Drink of it, all of you; for this is my blood" [Matthew 26:26-27].

To visit the eucharistic Lord in the tabernacles that are the Arks of the New Covenant is, thus, to return, time and again, to the One who liberates us in the deepest meaning of freedom: freedom from sin and death. May this unique book deepen the Church's eucharistic devotion and thereby empower the people of the Church for the mission of evangelization that Lynda Rozell carries out with such faith, hope, and love.

GEORGE WEIGEL, the biographer of Pope St. John Paul II, is Distinguished Senior Fellow of Washington's Ethics and Public Policy Center.

PROLOGUE

As infants, we grasp our parents' hands to pull up and walk, first with small faltering steps then constantly collapsing to the ground. We stumble yet grow ever more confident as toddlers until we run, perilously crashing into furniture and down stairs. Through childhood and into adulthood, we keep getting up and striding forward, sometimes slipping on black ice or tripping when we become distracted as we wander along the edges of cliffs. Yet, God is always there to guide us, to pick us up when we fall, to comfort and to strengthen us. He works through others and through the challenges and crosses that come our way, that we may become who He made us to be, one with Him in eternity. It is all love. It is all gift.

This book is about His love, His longing for us to return to Him. We are all on a journey, in freedom, to choose to be with Him. Our lives are a pilgrimage to our first and ultimate home in Heaven. As pilgrims, we receive food from Him for that journey, and He revives us with life-giving water to sustain us through Jesus Christ. God the Father revealed Himself in Jesus as the way for us to return to Him. Jesus, one with the Father and the Holy Spirit, the Creator of the Universe, is beyond time and space, yet He entered into them as a weak, vulnerable infant to bear the consequences of our sins and redeem us.

As a pilgrim on this journey, I seek out tabernacles. It is there that Jesus remains sacramentally present with us, in His Body, Blood, Soul, and Divinity, until we meet again. While God is with us all the time, in every place, including within the divine beauty of nature, the tabernacle is special. Receiving Jesus at Mass in Holy Communion is the pinnacle of the day; His Real Presence in a tabernacle is the next best thing. Quiet time before the tabernacle is as close as I can come to Jesus on this earth outside of Holy Communion. This intimacy with Him draws me back again and again despite my many failures and distractions.

Beyond an individual relationship with God, we all are called to invite others into communion with Him. In my case, I travel all over the United States in a van as a pilgrim and missionary.[1] God called me to become a nomad, to live on the road among other nomads, to work and volunteer with them. Through friendship and kindness, in small ways in my ordinary life at campsites and communities found on the road, I witness to God's love and the salvation Jesus won for us.

As I travel and visit tabernacles across the United States, I sense God's longing for his people. "Return to me" is something I hear in prayer and is a theme I often see in Scripture and spiritual reading. Rekindling faith in the True Presence of Christ in the Eucharist strengthens our relationship with Him and with one another as a body of believers. Inviting others to grow in their relationship with God is a way of loving my neighbors as myself. Love shared is love multiplied, not reduced as the number of participants each claim their own personal share. God is not a pie that diminishes as each

---

[1] *See* Rozell, Lynda. *Journeys with a Tin Can Pilgrim: From Corporate Lawyer to Airstream Nomad* (St. John's Press 2021), a spiritual travel memoir about how to grow closer to God, lead a simplified life, and travel in a truck and trailer.

person receives a slice. He remains beyond time and space, wonderfully and infinitely available, in intimate relationship with each and all.

This devotional for use in visiting Christ in the tabernacle comes out of my pilgrim travels. In addition, the National Eucharistic Revival movement sponsored by the United States Council of Catholic Bishops (henceforth, USCCB) nourished my desire to share Him with others. Launched in 2022 on the Feast of Corpus Christi (the Body and Blood of Christ), the revival seeks to "renew our worship of Jesus Christ in the Eucharist."[2] Despite scandal, division, and doubt, "Jesus is present, reminding us that he is more powerful than the storm. He desires to heal, renew, and unify the Church and the world."[3] Christ will unite us "once again around the source and summit of our faith in the celebration of the Eucharist."[4] With the inspiration of the Holy Spirit, the ongoing revival calls the faithful to go out on mission to share the gift of love for the Lord in the Eucharist with their parishes, families, friends, and others they encounter.[5]

We can all participate in that mission. The Holy Spirit prompts me to do my small part by offering this collection of photos, reflections, and prayers to touch others and help them draw close to our

---

[2] USCCB, National Eucharistic Revival website, "Jesus Is Calling Us Deeper" https://www.eucharisticrevival.org.

[3] *Id.*, "Why Now?" https://www.eucharisticrevival.org.

[4] *Id.*

[5] *See* USCCB, National Eucharistic Revival website, "National Eucharistic Revival," https://www.eucharisticrevival.org/mission-vision-and-timeline.

Eucharistic Lord and the love He offers. God calls everyone as disciples to share the Good News of salvation in our ordinary lives, whether we are single, married, consecrated priests or religious, and no matter what our circumstances. How can we plant seeds and cultivate a return to belief in the Real Presence and a return to Mass in person? We begin by renewing and reviving our own devotion to Christ in the Eucharist. One cannot give what one doesn't have.

When I visited tabernacles in my travels, I sought Jesus in His sacramental presence for private prayer and spiritual nourishment.[6] I wasn't planning to write a book about His Real Presence in tabernacles until fairly recently. Accordingly, this work is not a comprehensive study of all themes and design elements included in tabernacles. Instead, it reflects my experience as a nomad traveling the country but always finding a home in Christ. Unless otherwise stated, I visited and photographed each tabernacle included in this book. Tabernacle design and art often inspired my reflections as I sat before Jesus, listening to Him. Later, themes for the meditations in this book emerged from the photos I took in the churches where I spent time with Jesus in the Blessed Sacrament.

Many tabernacles contain multiple themes and symbols. The chapters that follow address the themes of Nourishment, Sacrifice, Jesus, Spirit, Church, and Mission. Each chapter provides some historical or theological background on a tabernacle theme. Next, it

---

[6] For a helpful guide to prayers of adoration in general, *see* Diocese of Arlington, "Come and Rest Awhile, A Guide to Praying with Jesus in the Blessed Sacrament, compiled by Women Religious in the Diocese of Arlington" (2021), https://www.arlingtondiocese.org/communications/adoration-guide-final.pdf.

Prologue

contains reflections on design elements and symbols of that theme and presents photographic examples. Each section addressing a tabernacle motif concludes with suggested prayers or devotions related to that motif. They range from well-known prayers to the more obscure and include some of my own composition. Think of them as icebreakers or conversation openers as you enter more deeply into your own conversation with Jesus in His sacramental presence.

You can read this book sequentially or select sections based on tabernacles you visit or what themes might inspire your prayer. Whether you already visit tabernacles regularly outside of Mass or a formal holy hour, or have never done so, my hope is that you will find inspiration and value in this book. May it help you to grow closer to Jesus in His Real Presence in the Blessed Sacrament.

Moreover, once you nourish your own relationship with Christ at the tabernacle, the love He gives you will overflow. You'll want to invite others to return to relationship with God, to recognize that they are His beloved sons and daughters. Ask Him to help and invite them to pray with you. Conversation with God through prayer leads to a longing for more intimacy with Him, a longing to return home. There are many resources available from the National Eucharistic Revival and elsewhere that you can share,[7] but outreach is more than an appeal to the intellect. It is spirit, and that spirit of love is what moves you and each of us to seek intimacy with Jesus. May this little

---

[7] *See, e.g.,* Eucharistic Symposium sponsored by the Diocese of Arlington, available with other resources on the diocesan website at https://www.arlingtondiocese.org/national-eucharistic-revival; events and resources available on the Diocese of Portland's website at https://portlanddiocese.org/eucharistic-revival-resources.

book about finding Him and accompanying Him in the tabernacle help you to stay in His presence everywhere and always so that your joy may light the way for others.

PART ONE

INTRODUCTION

CHAPTER ONE

Wonder and Awe

Jesus invites you to visit Him in the tabernacle at any time, not only when He is exposed on the altar for formal adoration. Tabernacle art and symbols can inspire your prayer and help you to focus on His Real Presence there. Come with me to explore how to grow in relationship with our Lord by reflecting on what we find at His dwelling place, the tabernacle. Let's start by approaching Him in your local church.

Imagine that the door swings open in the shimmering light of a hot summer day. Heat rising from the pavement makes every step an effort. Inside, coolness breathes a dance into diffuse streams of color pouring down from high windows. Beyond the rows of wooden seats, behind the gleaming white marble altar, a single candle glows. Its light flickers over an ornate domed box adorned with kneeling angels ensconced in a niche. There, He waits for us and for any and all who might seek His peace in this stillness.

Here, in this box and in countless others in churches around the world, resides the Lord of the Universe, the Maker of all things, dwelling silently within a thing made by the hands of His creations. This is the tabernacle, the dwelling place of God in His sacramental form, the Eucharist. The tabernacle is the home of the Beloved who chooses to stay close to us.

A tabernacle containing the Eucharist is the beating heart of a Catholic church.[1] It holds our greatest treasure — God Himself, humbly incarnate in the form of consecrated unleavened bread. As Blessed Carlo Acutis explains, Jesus remains with us wherever there is a consecrated host. There is no need to make pilgrimages to Jerusalem or other "places where Jesus lived 2000 years ago. . . Tabernacles ought to be visited with the same devotion!"[2]

The tabernacle encases, holds, reserves the Body and Blood of Jesus Christ in the form of sacred hosts with the outward appearance and characteristics of bread. In this Blessed Sacrament, Jesus literally remains with us, His children. He lets us see Him, touch Him, and consume Him so His life grows in us.

These wafers are more than meets the eye, more than what we hold in our hands, more than what we taste in our mouths. This food, the very substance of Christ, is the gift He ordained to feed and to strengthen our souls until we meet again. It is bread for the journey that we all are on to everlasting life in Him and with Him, the Father, and the Holy Spirit.

---

[1] *See* Catholic Church. *Catechism of the Catholic Church: Revised in Accordance with the Official Latin Text Promulgated by Pope John Paul II.* United States Catholic Conference, 2000 (hereinafter CCC) 1324 ("The Eucharist is the source and summit of the Christian life.") At every Mass, Jesus's one Sacrifice is made sacramentally present and offered to God under the forms of bread and wine. *See* CCC 1333; 1353-1355. *See also* Matt. 26:26-29; Luke 22:17-20. All citations to Scripture are to the USCCB online version of the New American Bible Revised Edition.

[2] Kunnappally, Ephrem. *Highway to Heaven: A Spiritual Journey through the Life of Blessed Carlo Acutis* (Pavanatma Publishers 2020) at 44-45.

How do we understand this mystery? Only through grace. Words fail to fully describe the Blessed Sacrament itself. The USCCB explains that:

> In the celebration of the Eucharist, bread and wine become the Body and Blood of Jesus Christ through the power of the Holy Spirit and the instrumentality of the priest. The whole Christ is truly present -- body, blood, soul, and divinity -- under the appearances of bread and wine, the glorified Christ who rose from the dead. This is what the Church means when she speaks of the "Real Presence" of Christ in the Eucharist.[3]

This isn't an intellectual concept or a metaphor or a symbol. It is a person offering us the most important relationship in our lives. From the greatest of theologians to the simplest of children's songs, many have tried to describe the Real Presence and their faith that this small humble piece of bread literally is fully Jesus. For example, Saint Thomas Aquinas in his beautiful hymn *Adoro Te Devote*[4] prays:

---

[3] USCCB, "The Eucharist," https://www.usccb.org/eucharist. *See also* CCC 1384 (the Blessed Sacrament is "the body and blood, together with the soul and divinity, of our Lord Jesus Christ and, therefore, the whole Christ is truly, really and substantially contained").

[4] *Adoro Te Devote* was composed at Pope Urban IV's request for use in the Corpus Christi Solemnity Mass that the Pope would establish in response to a Eucharistic miracle.

Seeing, touching, tasting are in thee deceived;
How says trusty hearing? that shall be believed;
What God's Son has told me, take for truth I do;
Truth Himself speaks truly or there's nothing true.[5]

In other words, Saint Thomas believes Jesus, who is truth, speaks the truth when Jesus says, "This is my body" and "This is my blood" at the Last Supper.

By contrast to Saint Thomas' soaring poetry, yet in the same spirit, I have heard little children joyfully sing a simple praise song "E-U-C-H-A-R-I-S-T." The song spells out the meaning of the Blessed Sacrament, that Jesus is tangibly present. For instance, C stands for "Christ is wholly and truly there in Tabernacles everywhere!"[6]

Children and saints can help us try to understand the mystery of the Eucharist. As Saint Thomas Aquinas found, however, the words of Jesus Himself remain the most instructive. In the Bread of Life discourse, Jesus plainly states: "I am the living bread that came down from heaven; whoever eats this bread will live forever; and the bread

---

[5] *Adoro Te Devote*—A Eucharistic Hymn by Saint Thomas Aquinas, translation by Gerard Manley Hopkins, Cathedral of the Immaculate Conception (Springfield IL) website, https://spicathedral.org/blog/adoro-te-devote-a-eucharistic-hymn.

[6] The Eucharist Song was written by Mary Zitnik and performed on her album *Totally Catholic MMXVII*. Copyright © Mary Zitnik. Quoted with permission. All rights reserved. The song is available on the website of Saint Martin of Tours Catholic Church in La Mesa, California, at http://stmartinoftoursparish.org/eucharist-song and also https://maryzitnik.com/track/584230/e-u-c-h-a-r-i-s-t.

that I will give is my flesh for the life of the world."[7] Jesus did not try to soften his description of the Eucharist so that people repelled and scandalized by the notion of eating his body and drinking his blood would not leave Him. He did not claim to be speaking in a parable or by metaphor or symbol. Instead, He used the specific word that refers to gnawing on meat when He responded, "Amen, amen, I say to you, unless you *eat* the flesh of the Son of Man and drink his blood, you do not have life within you."[8]

Jesus sacrificed Himself for love of us and in obedience to the Father's will. The Mass is the purpose and reason for the Church that brings us the Eucharist. In commenting upon the relationship between the Mass and eucharistic devotion, Father Edward McNamara clearly distinguishes one from the other: "The celebration of the holy sacrifice of the Mass is the center and focal point of the Church's life to which all other aspects, including those intimately bound up with celebration itself, must take second place."[9] He observes,

> [L]iturgical norms direct that when the tabernacle is present in the sanctuary a genuflection of adoration is made at the beginning of Mass before the priest kisses the altar and at the end after kissing the altar before leaving the sanctuary. But

---

[7] John 6:51.

[8] John 6:53.

[9] McNamara, Rev. Edward, "Where the Tabernacle Should Be," *Zenit Daily Dispatch* (Jan. 27, 2004), https://www.ewtn.com/catholicism/library/where-the-tabernacle-should-be-4377.

no genuflections are made to the tabernacle during the celebration of Mass itself except when the priest reserves consecrated hosts left over after Communion. Thus, full attention must be given to the celebration itself in each of its parts.[10]

These norms are consistent with the reality that celebration of the Mass makes Jesus really and truly, literally present with us through the consecration of the bread and wine. That Presence remains even after Mass. By storing the consecrated hosts in the tabernacle for later consumption, we keep Jesus tangibly with us in His Body and Blood, Soul and Divinity. He allows us in His mercy and humility to reserve His sacramental presence in the tabernacle.

Think of the Eucharist as the sacrament of love, as God present with us, Emmanuel here today and at the same time everywhere, in our hearts, in nature, in Heaven. As you'll see in the photographs this book contains, the boxes Jesus resides within vary in shape, size, design, materials, and location. Wherever they are, the living presence of Jesus dwells within them and waits for us in each church. We don't have to wait for a formal holy hour; we can visit Him on our own at the place where He remains with us. He longs for us to accept his invitation to come to Him.

Thus, not only can we receive the tremendous gift of the Real Presence in Holy Communion, but we can also draw close in prayer at any time, particularly by visiting the tabernacle where the Eucharist dwells. As we gaze at the tabernacle, we seek to find God within and engage Him in prayer.

---

[10] *Id.*

Reading this book will help you make a visit to the tabernacle by giving you ideas to bring to prayer. Why visit the tabernacle? After all, God is everywhere and you can pray anywhere, at any time. At the tabernacle, however, you pray in His sacramental presence, honoring and accompanying Him in person. Jesus is fully present there, body and soul, humanity and divinity, and He delights in your presence with Him.

Simply visiting the tabernacle is an act of love. We long to spend time with those we love. At the tabernacle, you give the Lord your undivided time and attention. It may be as simple as stopping for a few moments at a church on your way to school or work to say hello. You are checking in, as you might with your spouse or friend. Jesus doesn't demand that you have an agenda to spend time with Him. Tell Him about your day even though He already knows. Then, listen to Him, resting in His peace.[11] You may not receive an answer or direction that you detect, but you are being blessed by His sacramental presence. You are storing up His peace in your heart, like the cool depths of a lake where waves and wind stir the surface but do not disturb what lies beneath.

The art and symbolism of the tabernacle itself can spark your conversation with God or suggest themes for meditation. Prayer is a conversation with God, but sometimes we don't know what to say.

---

[11] "If he does not always respond with words communicated to the mind, he always responds with love communicated to the heart." Schneider, Victoria. *The Bishop of the Abandoned Tabernacle: Saint Manuel González García* (Scepter Publishers 2018) (private revelations and prayer about receiving Jesus at Mass more reverently and keeping Him company in the tabernacle), p. 96.

Like any visit to a loved one, a visit to the tabernacle can be a time for conversation or for silence, while simply enjoying each other's presence. Christian meditation is a form of silent prayer that "seeks not to empty the mind but to fill it by being open to the presence of God."[12] Through meditation, "a disciple of Christ contemplates Jesus's life and teachings with the aim of listening to God. Meditation seeks to better understand God to discern his will more clearly."[13]

The suggestions for prayer and meditation contained in this book should be viewed as icebreakers. Based on themes found in tabernacle art and design, they provide jumping off points for your own conversations with our Eucharistic Lord. The photographs and reflections in this devotional show you how to do this and offer you a way to focus again on Jesus in the tabernacle when your thoughts drift away.

Also, ask the Holy Spirit to pray for you and to help you pray. You may find yourself drawn to praying specifically for an intention, for a person you care about or who presents difficulty in your life, for guidance with a difficult decision. Familiar prayers like an Our Father, Hail Mary, or Glory Be can be said. Praying the Divine Mercy chaplet or a Rosary before a tabernacle offers the Lord your love in a form you easily can share with others present or in your own mind.

If you have time, you can set an alarm on your phone and pray your own holy hour (or holy half or quarter hour!). Some people read spiritual books in their time before the tabernacle. Others write

---

[12] Armenio, Rev. Peter V. *Highlights of the Catholic Faith* (Midwest Theological Forum 2023), p. 427.

[13] *Id.*

down their thoughts and reflections in journals. In its simplest and purest form, you look at Him and He looks at you. You rest in each other's presence. No words are necessary. Still, if your thoughts wander you can bring them back to worship by using some of the reflections and prayers contained in this book.

Finally, you may wish to end your visit by making a spiritual communion, something you can do at the tabernacle or elsewhere throughout the day. By this prayer, you ask to receive all the graces of the Sacrament spiritually at a time you are unable to receive in person through sacramental Communion. This spiritual communion prayer written by Saint Alphonsus Ligouri may already be familiar to you:

> My Jesus, I believe that You are present in the Most Blessed Sacrament. I love You above all things, and I desire to receive You into my soul. Since I cannot now receive you sacramentally, come at least spiritually into my heart. I embrace You as if you were already there, and I unite myself wholly to You. Never permit me to be separated from You.

The more you visit tabernacles, the more you perceive and rejoice in His Presence and the more grace you receive as you unite yourself with Him. Let's begin our journey to tabernacles together as pilgrims through the pages that follow.

CHAPTER TWO

History and Development of the Tabernacle

A tabernacle is a place where God dwells. The tabernacles I describe in the next part of this book are those built to contain the consecrated hosts reserved for later use. Such hosts are Jesus, fully present in the substance of what appears to our senses to be mere bread. The very purpose of the tabernacle is to secure, honor, and protect the Eucharist: the sacramental presence of Jesus.[1]

History helps us understand more fully how tabernacles came to be used and the meaning of tabernacle art. God chose to dwell in many different tabernacles throughout salvation history and today. The design, construction, and placement of tabernacles within a place of worship has changed over time, yet the tabernacle's role as custodian and protector of the Real Presence remains constant.

History of the Tabernacle

The original meaning of the word tabernacle in Latin conveys a hut or tent. In the Old Testament book of Exodus, the word *Tabernacle* was used to refer to the tent in which the Ark of the Covenant

---

[1] Jesus is fully present in the consecrated host and likewise is fully present in the consecrated wine. One need not receive both to receive Him in His Body and Blood, Soul and Divinity. Consecrated wine, because it may spoil due to its natural properties, is not kept in a tabernacle. Instead, it is fully consumed at the Mass. If any of this Precious Blood remains after Communion, the priest or a person he designates consumes it.

and other sacred objects were kept.[2] God directed construction of this tabernacle and its contents for Him to reside in among the Israelites during their journeys through the desert.[3] Later, in both the Old and New Testaments, devout Jews commemorated their dwelling in the desert in tents by constructing huts to live in for seven days during the feast of Booths or Tabernacles.[4] Today, many Jews continue this custom in the Festival of Sukkot, a time of rejoicing marked by construction of temporary four-sided structures with open roofs.[5]

At Timna Park, north of Eliat in Israel, a life-size replica of this biblical tabernacle exists. Within the tabernacle tent of the Old Testament, a veil suspended from four pillars created an inner sanctuary. This sanctuary, the Holy of Holies, contained the Ark of the Covenant, a lampstand, and a table for the bread of the presence, an offering to God in part reserved for nourishment of the priests.

The Old Testament Ark of the Covenant was made of gold. On top of it two gold cherubim stretched their wings to cover a propitiatory (a place of atonement and reconciliation, also called the mercy seat). The cherubims' bodies turned toward each other, with wing tips meeting over the mercy seat and faces gazing at the seat.[6] It was

---

[2] Schaefer, Reverend Francis. "The Tabernacle: Its History, Structure, and Custody," *American Ecclesiastical Review,* May 1935 at 449-468 https://www.catholicculture.org/culture/library/view.cfm?recnum=679; *see* Exod 33:25-31, 35-40.

[3] Exod 25:1-9; Exod 26:1-30.

[4] Schaefer, *supra* note 2.

[5] Zimmerman, Rabbi Jack. "Sukkot; The Feast of Booths" *Jewish Voice* (Dec. 1, 2015), https://www.jewishvoice.org.

[6] Exod 25:17-22.

Chapter Two: History and Development of the Tabernacle   15

at this seat where God was to meet Moses within the tabernacle tent. As the specific location of God's presence, the Ark was a tabernacle within a sanctuary within the larger tabernacle tent.

Photograph 1—Model of Old Testament Tabernacle, Timna Park, Israel. Creative Commons Attribution - ShareAlike 4.0 International, https://commons.wikipedia.org/wiki/user.Mboesch.

The Ark contained three items: manna in a gold jar, the tablets inscribed by God with the Ten Commandments, and Aaron's flowering staff that symbolized the priesthood.[7] Manna is the bread God provided to the Jews in the desert, to sustain them until they reached the land promised by God. In the New Testament, Jesus contrasts the manna that sustained human life temporarily to Himself as the Bread of Eternal Life. "I am the bread of life. Your ancestors ate the

---

[7] *See* Heb 9:4-5; Exod 25:16.

manna in the desert, but they died; this is the bread that comes down from heaven so that one may eat it and not die."[8] Jesus satisfies our hunger completely, forever, while manna fed the Jews for forty years in the desert.[9]

Just as the bread of the presence and manna prefigure Jesus, the Old Testament Ark prefigures the new Ark, Mary, as discussed in Chapter Nine. The blessed womb of Mary was the earliest tabernacle or dwelling place of Christ. She gave birth to the infant Jesus, the incarnate Son of God, in a stable in Bethlehem. The name Bethlehem means House of Bread, so one might view that little town itself as a tabernacle. In the stable, Mary laid Jesus in a manger as his first resting place outside of her womb. Remarkably, the manger also was a tabernacle, a container for holding food and feeding hungry animals. Think about that. There, in the House of Bread, in a feeding trough, God chose to reside as a vulnerable newborn infant who would become the Bread of Life for us.[10]

Tabernacles made of wood evoke that manger, as do those that literally depict Jesus in the manger. At Saint James Catholic Church in Potosi, Missouri, the tabernacle supports a sculpture of the baby Jesus in the manger. Reflect upon how the baby's small hands reach out to us, as his arms later will open to embrace us on the cross. That embrace He still offers through His eucharistic presence in the golden tabernacle.

---

[8] John 6:48-50.
[9] Josh 5:11-12; Exod 16:35.
[10] Rottman, Rev. Nicholas, "Born in Bethlehem – the 'House of Bread'" *Source and Summit* (Diocese of Covington, Oct. 13, 2020), https://covdio.org/born-in-bethlehem-the-house-of-bread.

Chapter Two: History and Development of the Tabernacle 17

As Christians, we too are living tabernacles of the Holy Spirit who dwells within us through grace. For a time after receiving Communion our bodies contain Christ in His sacramental presence until the host and wine are fully consumed through digestion. We become what we eat, nourished by the Bread of Life to live in and through Jesus with the Trinity. Like Him, we are called to stretch out our hands to others, like the baby in the manger, and to embrace them on the cross.

Photograph 2—St. James Catholic Church, Potosi, MO.
Used with permission.

Development of the Tabernacle in the Catholic Church

The very early Church gradually began using dedicated tabernacles. During Roman persecutions it appears that it was more common for Christians to keep consecrated particles of Eucharist in their homes rather than in set churches with a fixed tabernacle. This practice was to avoid having the Host vulnerable to being seized and desecrated by pagans.[11]

Photograph 3—Eucharistic Dove, French early 13th century, courtesy of The Walters Art Museum, Baltimore, MD. Creative Common License CC0

As of the fourth century, it became widespread practice to reserve the Host in churches. Receptacles holding the Host varied

---

[11] Schaefer, *supra* note 2.

Chapter Two: History and Development of the Tabernacle

greatly. They may have been inside niches in the walls of churches. One fairly common practice was to place the Eucharist inside a vessel in the shape of a dove, representing the Holy Spirit.[12] The dove in turn typically rested above the altar, suspended by chains from the ceiling of a canopy, or *baldacchino* (baldachin, in English). Early Christian churches commonly used such canopies, and many Catholic churches continue to do so today. Originally called *ciboria*, from the Greek *chiborion*,[13] gradually the term *baldacchino* came to be used for the architectural feature of a canopy-like roof made of wood or metal and supported by columns.[14] Saint Peter's Basilica in Rome boasts the largest and most famous baldacchino, adorned by the artist Bernini's massive twisting columns. The baldacchino remains a common feature today, as shown by the marble and mosaic example from Saint Joan of Arc Catholic Church in Indianapolis, Indiana.

Over time, the word *ciborium* came to mean the chalice or bowl that holds consecrated hosts. It typically has a cover and is made of metal. The ciborium retains consecrated hosts that remain after a Mass for later distribution at another Mass or communion service. The retained hosts also may be transferred to a pyx, a small box, to carry Jesus in His sacramental presence to the sick or homebound.

---

[12] *Id.*

[13] *Id.*

[14] Bianchi, Hanael. "Bernini's baldacchino is actually a ciborium," *Catholic Review* (Dec.2, 2020), https://catholicreview.org/berninis-baldacchino-is-actually-a-ciborium.

*Photograph 4—St. Joan of Arc Catholic Church, Indianapolis, IN.
Used with permission.*

Chapter Two: History and Development of the Tabernacle   21

In addition to a pyx, the tabernacle often contains a luna, a round receptacle with a clear glass front.[15] The luna can be inserted into a monstrance for adoration, eucharistic processions, Benediction or other devotions. The monstrance containing the luna makes the Blessed Sacrament visible to the adorers. The luna and monstrance may be quite large to accommodate a larger host that can be seen from a distance, as seen in this example from Saint Bernard's Catholic Church in Belfield, North Dakota.

Photograph 5—Monstrance at Altar of St. Bernard's Catholic Church, Belfield, ND. Used with permission.

---

[15] Van Sloun, Rev. Michael. "Tabernacles Inside and Outside of Church," *The Catholic Spirit* (Nov. 21, 2019), https://thecatholicspirit.com/faith/focus-on-faith/faith-fundamentals/tabernacles-inside-and-outside-of-church.

In addition to niches and doves in the fourth century, by the eleventh century the Eucharist sometimes dwelt within a gold or silver tower, placed or fastened on the altar or suspended with chains from a canopy. The doves holding the Eucharist may have been placed inside these towers.[16]

Another receptacle in which early Christians reserved the Eucharist was a Sacrament House or building made of stone that reached to the ceiling of the church. This eventually evolved into the locked box usually fixed at the center of the altar that came to be called a tabernacle by the end of the sixteenth century.[17]

In 1545, Catholic bishops met in Trent, Italy, to define Catholic doctrine and enact reforms in response to the rise of Protestantism. Following this Council of Trent, liturgical books and then canon law defined the placement and use of the tabernacle.[18] Because Protestant denominations in most instances came to deny the Real Presence of Christ in the Eucharist, Catholic churches began to place the tabernacle in a highly visible space, most often on a high altar on the back wall of the sanctuary.[19] By the mid-1800s, Sacrament

---

[16] Schaefer, *supra* note 2.

[17] *Id.*; *see also* Winters, Jaimie Julia. "Tabernacles change through time but have always been where God dwells," *Jersey Catholic* (March 28, 2023) https://jerseycatholic.org/tabernacles-change-through-time-but-have-always-been-where-god-dwells-photos-2.

[18] Schaefer, *supra* note 2.

[19] Dunn, Matthew. "The Prominence and Placement of Tabernacles Explained" (July 18, 2018), media.ascensionpress.com; Winters, *supra* note 17.

Chapter Two: History and Development of the Tabernacle

Houses and suspended pyxes no longer were used. Instead, the tabernacle was fixed to the altar along the back wall of the sanctuary.[20]

For most of the twentieth century, canon law specified that normally the Blessed Sacrament is reserved in only one place in the church and in the most prominent and honored space.[21] Almost always this continued to be on the main altar along the back wall of the church's sanctuary. Exceptions were allowed for circumstances where singers or many others would be moving around the altar, such as occurs in the celebration of certain devotions and in cathedrals, church colleges, and monasteries.[22]

With the Second Vatican Council (1962-1965), changes were made to reflect that the altar was the primary focus of the Mass, where the Liturgy of the Eucharist occurs. Kneeling, kissing, incensing, singing and consecration all take place at the main altar, requiring movement around it.[23]

By contrast, the tabernacle holds the already consecrated hosts and is more reflective, requiring stillness and silence around it. "The altar speaks to the senses while the tabernacle speaks to the heart," explains Father Robert Dente, liturgist and director of the Archdiocese of Newark's Worship Office. Therefore, he concludes it is preferable to separate the tabernacle from the altar on which Mass is celebrated.[24]

---

[20] Winters, *supra* note 17.
[21] *See* Code of Canon Law 1917, c.1111.
[22] Schaefer, *supra* note 2.
[23] Winters, *supra* note 17.
[24] *Id.*

Others do not find that there is any preference for location, so long as the tabernacle is prominent and easily visible.[25] The Catechism of the Catholic Church (CCC or Catechism) states that the tabernacle is to be situated "in churches in a most worthy place with the greatest honor. The dignity, placing, and security of the eucharistic tabernacle should foster adoration before the Lord really present in the Blessed Sacrament of the altar."[26] Similarly, current canon law specifies that the "Most Holy Eucharist is to be reserved habitually in only one tabernacle of a church or oratory…situated in some part of the church or oratory which is distinguished, conspicuous, beautifully decorated, and suitable for prayer."[27] Additionally, the tabernacle is to be "immovable, made of solid and opaque material, and locked in such a way that the danger of profanation is avoided as much as possible."[28] The Catechism further instructs that a tabernacle "should be constructed in such a way that it emphasizes and manifests the truth of the real presence of Christ in the Blessed Sacrament."[29]

After reviewing these and other sources, Ascension Press analyst Matthew Dunn concludes that "the church should use only one [permanent] tabernacle at a time" and observes that there is "no

---

[25] *See, e.g.*, Dunn, *supra* note 19.

[26] John Paul II, *Catechism of the Catholic Church*, 2nd ed., (Washington, DC: United States Catholic Conference, 2011), sec. 1183, https://www.usccb.org/sites/default/files/flipbooks/catechism/.

[27] Code of Canon Law 1983 (hereinafter abbreviated CIC), c. 938.

[28] *Id.*

[29] CCC 1379. *See* Hoffman, Rev. Francis, "Where Should the Tabernacle Be?" *Simply Catholic*, https://www.simplycatholic.com/where-should-the-tabernacle-be.

mention in either the Catechism or the Code of Canon Law about the tabernacle's location within the church."[30] He notes that the concept of a separate adoration chapel or tabernacles elsewhere than the altar did not exist before 1967 when the Vatican issued an instruction called *Eucharisticum Mysterium*.[31] Ultimately, he emphasizes, the tabernacle's location is left to the judgment of the diocesan bishop. The options Dunn identifies are the high altar, elsewhere in the church in a prominent place that is easy to find, or in an adoration chapel within the church building. He concludes that "[w]herever the tabernacle is, it needs to be prominent and not hidden."[32]

Keep this in mind as you search for tabernacles. Unfortunately, not all churches place the tabernacle in a prominent place that is easy to locate. As we shall see, there are many places to find the Real Presence of Jesus in the Eucharist.

---

[30] Dunn, *supra* note 19.
[31] The document is available at https://adoremus.org/1967/05/eucharisticum-mysterium.
[32] Dunn, *supra* note 19, quoting paragraph 314 of the General Instruction of the Roman Missal.

CHAPTER THREE

Where to Find Tabernacles

As pilgrims seeking to spend time with Jesus, we need to know where to find tabernacles. Any place in which Mass is regularly celebrated likely has one. I spend time before the tabernacle in small neighborhood churches, grand cathedrals, and chapels at monasteries, convents, colleges, and retreat centers.

If I can't find the tabernacle, I ask. Sadly, sometimes the tabernacle is not within the church, but is in a separate building. Once I found it in a tiny, unmarked closet-like room at the back of the church. Generally, however, the tabernacle is easy to find and centrally located at or near the main altar of a church, or nearby in a side chapel open to the main area of the Church, or in a clearly visible, separate chapel for private prayer.

In the sanctuary, the tabernacle may be on a high altar against the wall directly behind the altar table used for the Liturgy of the Eucharist, as shown below in the photograph of the Basilica of the Immaculate Conception in Jacksonville, Florida. It may be in an alcove or niche in the sanctuary, either behind the altar or to its side. For instance, at Saint Philip Catholic Church in Franklin, Tennessee, pictured in Chapter Six, a tabernacle resembling a burst of light is set into a wall to the right of the altar.

If a tabernacle is placed in a sacramental chapel for private prayer and reflection, the chapel should not only be suitable for private adoration and prayer, but also be "organically connected to the

Photograph 6—Basilica of the Immaculate Conception, Jacksonville, FL. Used with permission.

church and readily visible to the Christian faithful."[1] Some even have chapels completely behind the sanctuary so that the Blessed Sacrament can be adored quietly in the chapel but also be present at the center of the church behind the main altar. In these instances, the faithful can view the tabernacle from both the main church and the chapel.

Photographs 7 and 8—St. Anastasia Catholic Church, St. Augustine, FL. Used with permission.

Compare the two photographs of the adoration chapel and the sanctuary at Saint Anastasia Catholic Church in Saint Augustine, Florida.

---

[1] USCCB, General Instruction of the Roman Missal (2010) chap. 5, para. 315(b), https://www.usccb.org/prayer-and-worship/the-mass/general-instruction-of-the-roman-missal.

Keep in mind that you are searching for Jesus; you are looking for a person, not a thing. The tabernacle itself is not the goal of your pilgrimage but rather Christ Himself contained within. A lit tabernacle lamp signifies His Real Presence in the tabernacle.

It bears mentioning, however, that there is one period per year when Jesus is not in the usual church tabernacle. Because there is no Mass on Good Friday through the evening Easter Vigil Mass, sufficient hosts are consecrated at Holy Thursday Mass for use until Easter. During this period, the church tabernacle is empty, and the Blessed Sacrament instead is reserved in a private tabernacle at an altar of repose.

As part of the seven churches pilgrimage devotion on Holy Thursday, worshippers may visit these altars of repose to keep Jesus company during His sufferings in the Garden of Gethsemane. This journey weaves prayer and Scripture together with adoration of Jesus in the Blessed Sacrament.[2] If available near you, it is a beautiful way to visit our Lord when He is absent from your church's usual tabernacle.

Sometimes, there are multiple chapels and multiple tabernacles within one church, as in the magnificent Basilica of the National Shrine of the Immaculate Conception in Washington, D.C. There, the variety and inclusivity of the universal church expresses itself in individual chapels honoring Mary in her many appearances to different peoples.

---

[2] *See* Diocese of Arlington, *Holy Thursday 7 Churches Pilgrimage Adult Reflections,* https://www.arlingtondiocese.org/uploadedfiles/cda/pages/youth_ministry/young_adult_ministry/7cp_booklet_eng_adult2023crop.pdf.

Chapter Three: Where to Find Tabernacles 31

Photograph 9—"Chapel of the Blessed Sacrament," Basilica of the National Shrine of the Immaculate Conception, Washington, D.C. Photographer Lynda Rozell. Used with permission of the National Shrine, 2023.

Likewise, across the United States, tabernacles vary greatly. They may be square, rounded, carved like a globe, sculpted to look like a miniature building or a dove or flames, or they may be veiled. God rejoices in the beauty and diversity of His Creation. How wonderful that we can express that variety in religious art and particularly in functional art, that which reverently holds Christ's Precious Body and Blood in the form of consecrated hosts!

PART TWO

AT THE TABERNACLE

CHAPTER FOUR

Nourishment

Many tabernacles portray food as a way of expressing the nourishment the Blessed Sacrament provides. Depictions of bread and wine or their constituent parts of grain and grapes are common. Vines and grapes and sheaves, or grains of wheat, refer to the raw ingredients of the bread and wine that become the Body and Blood of Jesus in the Mass. Other tabernacles incorporate fish and loaves, calling to mind the miracle of the loaves and fishes where Jesus multiplied the small amount the disciples had brought to Him to feed the many.

Some tabernacles represent nourishment by metaphor, for example, by picturing the fountains of water from which deer long to drink as described in Psalm 42. By contrast, others literally depict the Blessed Sacrament through the chalice and hosts. Finally, tabernacles also express the theme of nourishment through portrayals of the first eucharistic meal: the institution of the Holy Mass during the Last Supper.

Whether abstract patterns, like stylized drops of red to depict blood or wine, or realistic sculpting of grapes and grain and holy vessels, these symbols of food and drink embody Jesus's promise that "my flesh is true food, and my blood is true drink." All of them call to mind how Jesus gives us Himself in the Mass to nourish our immortal souls and help us to grow in holiness through grace.

Photograph 10—Our Lady of the Lake, Mount Arlington, NJ. Used with permission.

Photograph 11—St. Francis Xavier Cabrini Catholic Church, Vassar, MI. Used with permission.

For example, the tabernacle at Our Lady of the Lake in Mount Arlington, New Jersey, shown above, juxtaposes blades of wheat and bunches of grapes with hosts and the chalice. Similarly, a colorful tabernacle at Saint Francis Xavier Catholic Church in Vassar, Michigan, uses the color red to indicate the Holy Spirit falling upon the tabernacle as a stylized dove. The red blends with orange in a cross bearing a white host and flanked by bread and a pitcher of wine incorporating the bright colors used on the dove and cross.

Even more abstractly, three drops of blood or wine adorn a silver tabernacle at Saint Charles Borromeo Catholic Church in Tacoma, Washington. The background recalls blades of wheat, suggesting our next motif: the ingredients of bread and wine.

Chapter Four: Nourishment 37

Photograph 12—St. Charles Borromeo Catholic Church, Tacoma, WA. Used with permission.

Grain and Grapes

Grain and grapes, the raw materials of bread and wine, frequently appear in tabernacle art. When I see depictions of grain and grapes, I think of how we participate in Christ's ongoing redemption of the world when we unite our sufferings with His.[1] The same is true of our work. The work of human hands transforms the fruits of the earth into bread and wine that the Holy Spirit, working through the hands of the priest, then transforms into the Body and Blood of Christ. Jesus allows us to harvest His fruits and create the food and drink He then blesses and shares with us as His very self, as true food and true drink. He thus draws us into His sacrifice to save and redeem us. When we offer our sacrifice, our work, to Him, He changes it into something miraculous. It becomes part of what He has and is doing in His redemption of us, re-presented at every Mass.

As I stop to visit tabernacles, I sometimes face a technical challenge in accepting His invitation. Many churches lock their doors immediately after daily Mass. For instance, I stopped at Holy Spirit Parish in Rock Springs, Wyoming, hoping to pray at the tabernacle, but the church was closed. One of the teachers at the adjacent school spotted me, and I asked if an adoration chapel was open. She kindly walked me through the school to the neighboring church, Our Lady of Sorrows, and showed me a small chapel with a delightful tabernacle. Sometimes, you need to search for Jesus, but finding Him is always worth the effort!

---

[1] Saint Paul writes, "Now I rejoice in my sufferings for your sake, and in my flesh I complete what is lacking in Christ's afflictions for the sake of his body, the church" (Col 1:24). When we "offer it up," Christ adds our sufferings to His, sanctifying them for the sake of others. What is "lacking" is our embrace of suffering for the sake of others.

Chapter Four: Nourishment 39

Photograph 13—Our Lady of Sorrows Catholic Church, Rock Springs, WY. Used with permission.

This lovely tabernacle at Our Lady of Sorrows Catholic Church harmoniously intertwines grapes, vines, and stalks of wheat with a small banner echoing the hymn of the angels proclaiming, "Sanctus,

Sanctus, Sanctus" (Holy, Holy, Holy). A small silver cross rests in the center of the large cross around which vines form the shape of a heart. The grape vines, like our Lord, hang on the cross to nourish us. Refreshed by prayer before this tabernacle, I left ready to continue my journey.

Photograph 14—Mary, Mother of God Chapel, San Pedro Spiritual Development Center, Winter Park, FL. Used with permission.

Often an unexpected stop will provide an encounter with the Eucharistic Lord. I made an unplanned visit to a retreat center in Winter Park, Florida, while my new camper van was in the shop for some warranty work. The Mary, Mother of God Chapel at San Pedro Spiritual Development Center contains a tabernacle with art that reflects the abundance of God's love.

There, wheat springs up from a chalice. Less distinct blades fade into the background. They suggest an endless field of wheat to nourish all of humanity. Likewise, rich full bunches of plump grapes seem to spill over beyond the edges of the tabernacle door into the distance where our eyes cannot perceive them.

Hundreds of miles away from that Florida retreat center, wheat predominates on the tabernacle at Saint Frances Xavier Cabrini Shrine in New York City. Located in upper Manhattan, on a hill overlooking the Hudson River, the shrine honors Mother Cabrini, the patron saint of immigrants. The tabernacle's blades of wheat seem to bend and bow in a breeze, as if frozen in time, their motion captured in a snapshot. It reminds me of the Holy Spirit whom we do not see but whose effects we recognize.[2] The wind blows where it will, spilling grain everywhere, sowing seeds, leaving sanctifying traces in our souls and the world around us.[3]

Prayer/Devotion

The heart formed by grape vines on the cross on the tabernacle from Our Lady of Sorrows makes me think of a prayer written by

---

[2] *See* discussion of tabernacles with a Spirit theme in Chapter Seven.
[3] *See* John 3:8.

Photograph 15—St. Frances Xavier Cabrini, New York City, NY. Used with permission.

Saint Josemaria Escriva, founder of Opus Dei, as part of his meditations on the Way of the Cross. In commenting on how Saint Simon of Cyrene is forced to help Jesus carry the Cross, Saint Josemaria compares this to crosses we experience in our own lives: "At times the Cross appears without our looking for it: it is Christ who is seeking us out. And if by chance, before this unexpected Cross which, perhaps, is therefore more difficult to understand, your heart were to show repugnance... don't give it consolations. And, filled with a noble compassion, when it asks for them, say to it slowly, as one speaking in confidence: 'Heart: heart on the Cross! Heart on the Cross!'"[4] It is better to embrace with love the sufferings that come our way in life and ask Jesus to bear them with us and for us, on His Cross. He redeemed us once and for all in His one sacrifice, but we can offer Him our sacrifices and sufferings to use in that redemption.

The small cross in the middle of the larger cross also reminds me of how Jesus helps us bear our crosses in union with Him. Place your crosses at the foot of His Cross so that He may lift them up to the Father with you. In this way, His love sustains and strengthens our hearts as we face the sorrows and sufferings we encounter in our own lives.

You may wish to pray about the wheat or grapes you find in your own life and to thank God for them. Here's what came to mind for me:

> Lord, I stand in a field of grass heavy laden with seed. Your Spirit moves around me, making patterns, ripples, and waves in the swaying stalks of wheat. Gather me, Lord, as You gather Your grain; transform me into the person You made

---

[4] Escriva, Saint Josemaria. "Fifth Station: Simon of Cyrene helps Jesus to carry the Cross," *The Way of the Cross* (Scepter Publishers 1981).

me to be; let me be docile to Your Will, bending and surrendering to the wind, whether blasts of storms or gentle breezes. Holy Spirit living within me, make me food as well to nourish those around me by bringing Christ to them that we may all rejoice together in His harvest. Amen.

Loaves and Fishes

A tabernacle within a tabernacle nourished my soul in a side chapel at Saint Thomas Catholic Church in Staten Island, New York.[5] Inside a beautiful tabernacle shaped like a globe[6] a more traditional box bore an image of a basket of bread partially encircled by a fish. Bread for the world indeed!

The art inspired me to review the Gospel accounts of the miracle of the loaves and fishes. All four Gospels describe how Jesus fed crowds with a few loaves of bread and a couple of fish. After hearing of John the Baptist's death, Jesus withdraws by boat to a deserted place. He heals and preaches to the crowds that meet him there. In John's Gospel, Jesus asks Philip where Philip can go to buy food to feed the people, and Philip responds that there is not enough money for all to have even a little. Andrew then brings Jesus some food a boy offers, two fish and five barley loaves. Jesus gives thanks, breaks the bread, and returns the food to the disciples to feed the crowds.

---

[5] This tabernacle recently was moved to a repository of church art for the Archdiocese of New York, according to the priest who gave me a tour of Saint Thomas Catholic Church when I visited in 2019.

[6] *See* Chapter Nine for a photograph and discussion of the outer tabernacle shaped like a globe.

Chapter Four: Nourishment   45

After all have eaten and "have their fill," Jesus instructs the disciples to "gather the fragments left over so that nothing will be wasted."[7]

Photograph 16—St. Thomas Catholic Church, Staten Island, NY. Used with permission.

---

[7] John 6:12-13.

In the other Gospels, the disciples urge Jesus to tell the crowds to go away to the villages to find food, but Jesus instructs the disciples to "give the people some food yourselves."[8] The disciples give Jesus all they have, five loaves and two fish. He gives thanks, breaks the bread, and feeds the multitudes. In all four Gospels, twelve wicker baskets of fragments remain after feeding 5,000 men and their families.[9] In addition, the Gospels of Matthew and Mark reveal there was another time Jesus fed 4,000 men with seven loaves and a few fish.[10] On this occasion as well, the disciples collected the fragments of bread after everyone had eaten, filling seven baskets.[11]

So, when we see loaves and fishes on a tabernacle, we can reflect on how Jesus ultimately not only gives us Himself to eat, but also calls us to give of ourselves to others. Like the disciples, we are to share all that we have in imitation of Christ. To do so, we must become as children, trusting God to make the most of the little we have to offer.

Tabernacles with loaves and fishes remind us also to give thanks. Jesus looks up to heaven and thanks God before distributing the food. Through His actions, Jesus teaches us to thank God in advance for the miracles and gifts He gives us. We thank God in advance for our being able to receive Jesus truly present in Holy Communion and for the graces provided through that sacrament. By giving thanks before the miracle occurs, we honor God with our trust and faith in His promises.

---

[8] Luke 9:12-17; *see* Matt 14:15-18.
[9] Matt 14:20-21; Mark 6:34-44; Luke 9:17; John 6:13.
[10] Matt 15:32-38; Mark 8:1-9.
[11] Matt 15:37; Mark 8:8.

Also, consider that after the crowds eat their fill of fish and bread, the disciples gather the leftover pieces in baskets. The tabernacle is like a basket containing what is left after consecration and the feeding of the crowd during Communion. What remains is holy and is treated with respect, to be served again and not wasted.

Prayer/Devotion

Thank God for the abundance He provides to nourish us, to fill us with His grace. You may wish to use one of the following prayers or your own words. The first prayer comes from a website containing both traditional and original Catholic prayers:

> I thank You, Divine Redeemer, for coming upon the earth for our sake, and for instituting this adorable Sacrament in order to remain with us until the end of the world. I thank You for hiding beneath the Eucharistic species Your infinite majesty and beauty, which Your angels delight to behold, so that I might have courage to approach the throne of Your mercy. I thank You, most loving Jesus, for having made Yourself my food, and for resting upon this tongue, which has so often offended You, and for entering this body, which has so often deserved to be visited with Your anger. I thank You for uniting me to Yourself with so much love in this most wonderful Sacrament that I may live in You. [12]

---

[12] Castagnoli, Christopher. "A Prayer of Thanksgiving After Communion," *Our Catholic Prayers,* https://www.ourcatholicprayers.com/

Next, these words came to my mind at my visit to the loaves and fishes tabernacle in Staten Island:

> My Lord and my God, I love You, adore You, and thank You for Your many blessings. You cannot be outdone in generosity. Like the loaves and fishes, You multiply the gifts I bring to You. Your overflowing abundance fills me when I have nothing, when I'm tired or hungry, in body, mind or spirit. May I always trust Your enduring love, Your all-knowing Providence, in good times and in bad, trusting in You always as You see beyond my limits and know what is best for me. Let me abandon myself to Your divine plans for me, for goodness beyond imagining. In Jesus's name I pray as He taught us: [Our Father…] Amen.

Deer at a Fountain

Another tabernacle theme expressing nourishment echoes one of my favorite psalms and a hymn based on that psalm. As I drive, I often pray or sing to stay alert and make good use of time. Psalm 42:2-3 expresses the psalmist's longing to be with Christ, to worship and find refuge in Him:

> As the deer longs for streams of water,
> so my soul longs for you, O God.
> My soul thirsts for God, the living God.
> When can I enter and see the face of God?

---

thanksgiving-after-communion.html. The full prayer continues to thank Jesus for offering Himself as a sacrifice.

Chapter Four: Nourishment

Photograph 17—Blessed Sacrament Catholic Church, Clermont, FL. Used with permission.

The beautiful hymn "As the Deer Longs," based on this psalm, repeats, "As the deer longs for running streams so I long ... for you."[13] These words resonate with the image of water streaming forth from a fountain satisfying the deer's thirst. I'm especially delighted, then, when I find a tabernacle depicting deer at a fountain.

At Blessed Sacrament Catholic Church in Clermont, Florida, the tabernacle displays a fountain overflowing with water from which birds and deer drink. Deer at a fountain represent the creatures drawn to water needed to sustain them, and the fountain represents the living water that Christ provides to sustain us. In the Gospel of John, Jesus promises that "whoever drinks the water I give them will never thirst. . . the water I give them will become in them a spring of water welling up to eternal life."[14] Water also represents the Holy Spirit.[15]

The vivid imagery of Psalm 42 springs from the mourning of the Israelites in exile, far from the temple in Jerusalem that contains God's presence.[16] For those experiencing depression, those whose

---

[13] As the Deer Longs © 1988, Bob Hurd. Published by OCP. All rights reserved. Used with permission. Lyrics available at https://www.ocp.org/en-us/songs/1875/as-the-deer-longs; *see also* https://www.youtube.com/watch?v=06-vujlewQM&ab_channel=NewSongWirral (performance).

[14] John 4:14.

[15] In John 7:37-39 Jesus tells the crowd, "Let anyone who thirsts come to me and drink. Whoever believes in me, as scripture says: 'Rivers of living water will flow from within him.' He said this in reference to the Spirit that those who came to believe in him were to receive."

[16] *See* USCCB, note a to Psalm 42:2, https://bible.usccb.org/bible/psalms/42 (explaining that the term "the face of God" in the psalm refers to the personal presence of God in the Temple).

Chapter Four: Nourishment

souls are downcast, who long for happier days, the psalm offers hope.[17] Likewise, tabernacles with overflowing fountains remind us of that hope.

Prayer/Devotion

Jesus calls all to come to Him.[18] Sit with your pain before the tabernacle and accept the hope Christ offers. God remains the rock we cling to as torrents and waves sweep over us, as we struggle in the deep. "Deep calls to deep," the psalmist reminds us,[19] and the Lord hears us when we bring our pain to Him. As a deer is drawn to streams of water, we are drawn to the life Christ renews in us at Mass and before the tabernacle.

A deer is meek and mild, yet a wild, free creature. We, too, are free to make the choices that lead us toward or away from the living water. Reflect on how you are like the deer who is invited by the scent of freshness, the softness of ferns growing by the stream, the musical rush of water running along rock and splashing amid boulders.

What calls you to Christ? Will you offer Him your thirst and your sadness so He can satisfy and sustain you? Let your sorrow and suffering be boulders worn away and overcome by the living water Christ provides. Remember that He promises, "I will freely give water from the life-giving fountain to everyone who is thirsty."[20] Let

---

[17] Ps 42:12.
[18] *See* John 7:37-38.
[19] Ps 42:8.
[20] Rev 21:6.

yourself draw near to the overflowing fountain of grace at the tabernacle, so that Jesus may quench your thirst. He alone can fulfill that yearning.

As you sit or kneel before the tabernacle, imagine the grace of God like a river overflowing from it and running toward you. You may want to read Revelation 22:1 which uses images of water flowing from the throne of God and the Lamb in Heaven. Listen for the voice of Jesus as you imagine the flowing water. As He told the Samaritan woman seeking water at the well, He is the fountain of living water, the source of life.[21]

Reflect on how Jesus is essential to your life both naturally and spiritually. He will never abandon you. Instead, He awaits you longingly in the tabernacle. Thank Him for His gift of Himself in the Blessed Sacrament contained therein.

The Blessed Sacrament

Some tabernacles literally depict what they contain: the Blessed Sacrament. Images of the host and chalice cry out, "Here I am…the Body and Blood of Christ." Detailed portrayals often incorporate other symbols of eucharistic devotion.

For example, on the golden tabernacle at Mission San Luis Obispo de Tolosa Pro Cathedral in San Luis Obispo, California, angels offer the host and chalice beneath the cross, surrounded by rays of light spreading from a flaming sun. The tabernacle door's top and

---

[21] *See* John 4:13-14.

Chapter Four: Nourishment 53

bottom borders contain stylized waves of water surrounding the alpha and omega symbols.[22]

Photograph 18—Mission San Luis Obispo de Tolosa Pro Cathedral, San Luis Obispo, CA. Used with permission.

Contrast that tabernacle with a very simple colorful tabernacle on the other side of the country at Saint Philip Catholic Church in

---

[22] *See* discussion of alpha and omega in Chapter Six.

Auburn, Maine. There, the tabernacle depicts the Blessed Sacrament in mosaic form. Three hosts float above a chalice surrounded by light on a dark background. The use of three hosts evokes the Holy Trinity. The color red represents the Holy Spirit.

Photograph 19—St. Philip Catholic Church, Auburn, ME. Used with permission.

Fittingly, the church that Catholic author Flannery O'Connor attended near her home in Georgia contains a tabernacle showing the Blessed Sacrament. The entire focus of this smooth gold tabernacle is a simple single host that seems to emerge from a slender chalice. A cross rises from the smaller of two concentric mounds on top of the cylindrical tabernacle, suggesting the hill at Calvary. Angels kneel at either side of the tabernacle. Finely-embroidered images of the host and chalice, grapes and wheat, and the name of Jesus in a Christogram [23] decorate linens that cover the altar supporting the tabernacle. (I've placed this photograph below with a reflection based on Flannery O'Connor's famous remark regarding the Eucharist).

Prayer/Devotion

Reflect on how the Eucharist and Precious Blood are not symbols or metaphors, but the Real Body and Blood, Soul and Divinity of Christ. How would you explain the difference to a friend? Ponder in your heart two very different descriptions of this wondrous mystery.

First, Flannery O'Connor famously once blurted out at a dinner party, in response to novelist Mary McCarthy's comment that the Eucharist is a "pretty good" symbol, "If it's just a symbol, to hell with it!" She later wrote "That was all the defense I was capable of, but I realize now that this is all I will ever be able to say about it, outside of a story, except that it is the center of existence for me; all the rest of life is expendable." [24]

---

[23] See discussion of Christograms in Chapter Six.

[24] Fitzgerald, Sally, Editor. *Letters of Flannery O'Connor: The Habit of Being* (Farrar, Straus and Giroux, 1988) at 125.

Photograph 20—Sacred Heart Catholic Church, Milledgeville, GA. Used with permission.

Second, a beautiful contemporary reflection on the Eucharist comes from Sister Kathryn J. Hermes on the National Eucharistic Revival blog: "In the Eucharist we don't simply *remember* what Jesus did. In the Eucharist we *enter*, right now, *into* that reality with our entire being. In the Eucharist we *participate* in the salvation Jesus is

Chapter Four: Nourishment

bringing about on Earth today. The very flesh that Jesus received from the Virgin Mary on the day she said her *fiat* to the angel, the very flesh of the Child lying in the manger, is the same flesh that Jesus continues to give us sacramentally in the Eucharist.[25]

Last Supper

As you visit tabernacles to contemplate the Eucharist, you'll likely come across one that portrays the Last Supper. This motif in tabernacle art usually shows us Jesus with the men He chose to be the first priests and first bishops of the church, His apostles. He celebrates the first Mass, the meal He fervently longed to eat with them,[26] and institutes the Sacrament of the Eucharist. At this table in the upper room, Jesus proclaims, "This is my Body" and "This is my Blood," and then shares the bread and wine that become His very self. That Passover night, a night unlike all other nights, He commissions the apostles to do this in remembrance of Him.[27]

At American Martyrs Catholic Church in Manhattan Beach, California, the tabernacle depicts the apostles gathered around Jesus as He blesses the bread and a chalice of wine. Judas is in the background to the left, the only one without a halo. The table has plates, bread, and another cup on it. Within this portrayal of the Last Supper, we can pick different apostles to meditate on what it was like for

---

[25] Hermes, Kathryn J. "God has come to seek me out" *National Eucharistic Revival Blog* (Dec. 20, 2022), https://www.eucharisticrevival.org/post/god-has-come-to-seek-me-out.

[26] Luke 22:15.

[27] Luke 22:19-20.

them to be present at this sacred meal. We can place ourselves in the historical scene which stands outside of time and is re-presented at each Mass. Jesus, through the priest, offers you His body and blood. This is the supernatural reality behind what we perceive with our natural senses.

Photograph 21—American Martyrs Catholic Church, Manhattan Beach, CA. Photograph courtesy of American Martyrs Catholic Church. Used with permission. All rights reserved.

Prayer/Devotion

Tabernacles depicting the Last Supper inspire me to pray for vocations to the priesthood so that we may always have access to the

Eucharist at Mass and in tabernacles throughout the world. We cannot have the Blessed Sacrament without priests to consecrate it as Jesus directed. Here are some suggested prayers:

Prayer for Vocations Before the Blessed Sacrament

O Jesus, truly present in the Blessed Sacrament, draw all people to yourself, especially those you are calling to the priesthood and consecrated life. Give your Church, we pray, fervent priests to serve at your altar, and holy men and women who will devote their lives to prayer and service as consecrated brothers and sisters.

May the Heart of Jesus in the Most Blessed Sacrament be praised, adored, and loved with grateful affection at every moment in all the tabernacles of the world, even until the end of time. Amen. [28]

A Prayer for Priests by John Cardinal O'Connor (March 1995)

Lord Jesus, we your people pray to You for our priests. You have given them to us for OUR needs. We pray for them in THEIR needs.

---

[28] Copyright Vianney Vocations, used with permission. This Prayer for Vocations before the Blessed Sacrament comes from Vianney Vocations, a ministry devoted to renewing the Church by inspiring vocations to the priesthood and religious life. The prayer is available on their Eucharistic Revival card at https://vianneyvocations.com/product/prayer-card-blessed-sacrament.

We know that You have made them priests in the likeness of your own priesthood. You have consecrated them, set them aside, anointed them, filled them with the Holy Spirit, appointed them to teach, to preach, to minister, to console, to forgive, and to feed us with Your Body and Blood.

Yet we know, too, that they are one with us and share our human weaknesses. We know too that they are tempted to sin and discouragement as are we, needing to be ministered to, as do we, to be consoled and forgiven, as do we. Indeed, we thank You for choosing them from among us, so that they understand us as we understand them, suffer with us and rejoice with us, worry with us and trust with us, share our beings, our lives, our faith.

We ask that You give them this day the gift You gave Your chosen ones on the way to Emmaus: Your presence in their hearts, Your holiness in their souls, Your joy in their spirits. And let them see You face to face in the breaking of the eucharistic bread.

We pray to You, O Lord, through Mary the mother of all priests, for Your priests and for ours. Amen. [29]

---

[29] O'Connor, John Cardinal, Pontifical North American College website at https://www.pnac.org/support/prayers-for-seminarians/ Copyright © Pontifical North American College 2023. Used with permission. All Rights Reserved.

CHAPTER FIVE

Sacrifice

As we move with Jesus from His institution of the Eucharist at the Last Supper to the cross on Calvary, we ponder how the Eucharist is both nourishment and sacrifice. Mentally, we travel to the cross sustained by the true food and true drink given to us by Jesus. He gives us strength to contemplate and to enter into His sacrifice.

The cross is the most well-recognized symbol of Christianity. Not surprisingly, it also is the motif that appears most frequently on tabernacles. Crosses testify to Jesus's sacrifice and the salvation He won for us through His obedience to God's plan. They all speak love, but vary quite a bit in design and details. Crosses on tabernacles may be stylized or realistic. Those constructed of wood evoke Jesus's cross more strongly in their material.

At Saint Joseph on the Rio Grande in Albuquerque, New Mexico, for example, five red gemstones on the tabernacle's wooden cross abstractly represent the wounds of Jesus on the cross: the crown of thorns around His head, the nails in His hands and feet, and the spear that pierced His side. A stylized sun rises from the wooden canopy over the tabernacle supported by four columns. The sun reminds us that Jesus is the Light of the World, while its rounded rays complement the rope-like spiral design of the Solomonic columns.

Stylized crosses may be seen on many of the tabernacles pictured in this book. For example, the golden tabernacle at Saint Peter the Fisherman Catholic Church in Big Pine Key, Florida, bears a small

Photograph 22—St. Joseph on the Rio Grande, Albuquerque, NM. Used with permission.

cross on top of a fluted domed roof as well as a larger one in the center of the door on its cylindrical body. Yet another small cross rests in the center of the larger cross. Angels kneel before the crosses on the tabernacle door. Beams of light radiate from the sun behind the large cross. Fleurs-de-lis symbolizing the Trinity surround the

Chapter Five: Sacrifice   63

domed top of the tabernacle, suggesting a crown. They represent the crown of thorns and the crown of royalty, reminding us that Christ is the King of Kings who suffered for us.

Photograph 23—St. Peter the Fisherman Catholic Church, Big Pine Key, FL. Used with permission.

Crosses remind us that the Mass that brings us the Eucharist is more than a meal or celebration. The Mass re-presents the generous self-sacrifice of Jesus that opens the doors of Heaven to us. The theme of sacrifice also speaks occasionally through images of animals such as the pelican and the lamb, as we'll see in the pages that follow.

The Pelican

Legend has it that the pelican feeds its nestlings with blood from its own breast in times of drought and starvation. Christian art portraying the pelican as a symbol of Christ's sacrifice dates to the second century, but the legend predates Christianity.[1] Not only is the sacrificial, life-giving pelican found in art in many churches and tabernacles, Dante, Shakespeare, and Saint Thomas Aquinas refer to the legend in describing Christ's sacrifice.[2]

In the pelican theme, the baby birds represent us, the nest encircling them represents the church, and the mother pelican represents Christ as head of the church. Just as a sharp lance pierces Jesus's side as He hangs on the cross, the sharp beak of the mother pelican pierces its breast. The Blood of Christ feeds us; the blood of the mother pelican sustains her children. The mother sacrifices her life that her babies may live; Christ sacrificed His life so that we could

---

[1] Saunders, Rev. William. "What is the Symbolism of the Pelican Feeding Little Pelicans?" *Catholic Straight Answers*, https://catholic-straightanswers.com/what-is-the-symbolism-of-the-pelican-feeding-little-pelicans.

[2] *Id.*

Chapter Five: Sacrifice 65

live. In both instances, blood saves the lives of those receiving it. Thus, the mother pelican and her nestlings represent the Eucharist, redemption, and salvation.[3]

Photograph 24—St. Patrick Catholic Church, Miami Beach, FL. Photograph by James Dwight Davis ©. Used with permission. All rights reserved.

---

[3] Van Sloun, Rev. Michael, "Why the Pelican with Chicks Is a Symbol of the Eucharist," *Catholic Spirit*, (Jan. 23, 2019), https://thecatholicspirit.com/faith/focus-on-faith/faith-fundamentals/why-the-pelican-with-chicks-is-a-symbol-of-the-eucharist.

As you visit churches, you may find pelican art on the altar, in stained glass windows, and in other works. In Saint Patrick Church in Miami Beach, Florida, the symbols for the four evangelists mark the corners of a fine pelican tabernacle. The center contains a pelican feeding its chicks by drawing blood from its breast, a classical representation of the theme of sacrifice. Grapes and vines surround the pelican's nest, referencing the Precious Blood. Beams of light radiate from the pelican, representing the Holy Spirit.

Similarly, at Saint Anne's Catholic Church in Gorham, Maine, the pelican theme is combined with many other symbols. Here, the pelican is literally on a cross that bears the instruments of Christ's passion on the edges of the beams. As the mother pelican feeds its three nestlings with drops of blood running from her breast, we also can contemplate the crown of thorns, the nails, the scourges, the lance that Christ suffered for us. In addition, grapevines climb along the sides of the tabernacle up to the symbols of the alpha and omega.

The top of this tabernacle looks like a helmet or crown bordered with points of fleurs-de-lis, symbols of the Trinity. The helmet reminds us that when we receive Christ in the Eucharist we "put on the armor of God" to protect us in the battle against evil. Indeed, Saint Paul urges his readers to "take the helmet of salvation and the sword of the Spirit, which is the word of God" to fight against wickedness.[4] On top of the tabernacle's helmet, blades of grass form a plume gathered tightly like sheaves. They bring to mind the food of

---

[4] Eph 6:10-18.

Chapter Five: Sacrifice   67

grazing animals such as sheep and remind us that God provides for our needs.[5]

*Photograph 25—St. Anne's Catholic Church, Gorham, ME.
Used with permission.*

---

[5] *See* Matt 6:30 (even the grass of the field is clothed in beauty by God's care).

The pelican image may strike you as graphic. Yet, Christ's suffering and torture through the crucifixion also was bloody and graphic. He truly gave His blood and body to save us, and that sacrifice is eternally present in every Mass.

Prayer/Devotion

Lord, we thank you for nourishing us as your children and for giving us the Church to protect us and provide a home for us. Fed and strengthened by your sacramental presence, may we learn to fly, to go out into the world bearing your love to others.

Read and reflect upon the English translation of the hymn *Adoro Te Devote*, by Saint Thomas Aquinas. You'll find it in many hymnals or online.[6] Each stanza provides rich material explaining the eucharistic mystery. The pelican stanza, as translated by English poet Gerard Manley Hopkins, reads:

Like what tender tales tell of the Pelican
Bathe me, Jesus Lord, in what Thy Bosom ran
Blood that but one drop of has the pow'r to win
All the world forgiveness of its world of sin.

---

[6] *See, e.g.,* Hymnary.org, "Godhead here in hiding," https://hymnary.org/text/godhead_here_in_hiding; Word on Fire Institute, *Adoro Te Devote*, translated by Gerard Manley Hopkins and read by Jonathan Roumie (June 22, 2022), https://youtu.be/nItzkIJL7JM? si=MioTZfRmRlmOffo1.

The Lamb

The Lamb is perhaps the best-known symbol of Christ other than the cross. John identifies Jesus as the Messiah, the Lamb of God, whose sacrifice takes away the sins of the world.[7] Saint Paul confirms that "our paschal Lamb, Christ, has been sacrificed."[8] We are redeemed, says Saint Peter, "not with perishable things like silver or gold but with the precious blood of Christ as of a spotless unblemished lamb."[9]

At every Mass, after the consecration and before Communion is offered, Catholics pray the *Agnus Dei*, "Lamb of God who takes away the sins of the world, have mercy on us." When the priest invites us to Communion by elevating the consecrated host and chalice, his prayer synthesizes the sacrificial and salvific nature of Jesus's Real Presence: "Behold the Lamb of God, behold him who takes away the sins of the world. Blessed are those called to the supper of the Lamb."

In the Old Testament we find that lambs are sacrificed as early as Genesis. Abel offers the best of his flock, the first born, to the Lord for sacrifice.[10] The blood of the lamb sacrificed for the last meal the Jews eat in Egypt before fleeing marks the doors of God's people. This blood protects them from the Angel of Death who passes over their dwellings to strike the Egyptians' first born.[11]

---

[7] John 1:29-34.
[8] 1 Cor 5:7.
[9] 1 Pet 1:18-19.
[10] Gen 4:4.
[11] Exod 12:21-23.

In commemoration of God saving the Jews from slavery in Egypt, devout Jews, including Jesus, made a pilgrimage to Jerusalem each year to celebrate the Passover feast. As part of that feast, an unblemished lamb was sacrificed and eaten in the manner specified by the law. Indeed, the sacrificial lamb under the old law is a type of Jesus. Think of types as rough drafts or sketches that foreshadow something or someone yet to come.[12] All the sacrifices in the Old Testament foreshadow Christ, the one, complete, and only perfect sacrifice.

As theologian Marcellino D'Ambrosio explains, "[i]t was no accident that Jesus was arrested and put to death during Passover. In the Gospel of John, Jesus breathes his last at the very same moment that the Passover lambs were being sacrificed in the Temple."[13] He adds that John also emphasizes the fulfillment of Old Testament Scripture by the method the Romans used to confirm Jesus's death. Instead of breaking the legs of the crucified, as was customary, they thrust a lance into Jesus's heart.[14] Even this final indignity corresponds with the requirement that no bone of the Passover lamb be broken.[15]

---

[12] *See* Kelly, Mark J. "That Moses Thing," *Catholic Answers Magazine* (Sept 1, 2000), https://www.catholic.com/magazine/print-edition/that-moses-thing.

[13] D'Ambrosio, Marcellino. "Behold the Lamb of God: Reflection for the Second Sunday in Ordinary Time, *Catholic Mom Holy Cross Family Ministries*," (January 14, 2017), https://www.catholicmom.com/articles/2017/01/14/behold-lamb-god-reflection-second-sunday-ordinary-time.

[14] *Id.*

[15] *Id.*, citing Exod 12:46.

Chapter Five: Sacrifice

In addition to sacrifice, the lamb symbolizes meekness, gentleness, docility, innocence, and purity. Docility is being receptive to doing the will of God. Jesus knew what the sacrifice necessary for salvation of humankind would cost. He literally sweated blood in anticipation as He asked His Father to take this burden from Him, yet surrendered fully to His Father's will. The prophet Isaiah describes the Suffering Servant of the Lord as a lamb willingly led to sacrifice to free us from evil.[16] Further, those who seek to follow Jesus must do as He does. In the Gospel of Luke, Jesus sends his disciples out like "lambs among wolves"[17] to preach and heal.

Recalling the docility of Jesus, a reclining Lamb decorates the front of the tabernacle at Sacred Heart Parish in Colorado Springs, Colorado. This folk-art style tabernacle displays the Lamb with rays of light emerging from a halo around its head. Stylized flowers and leaves surround the tabernacle door. A pyramid rises from the top of the tabernacle to hold a cross.

The serenity of this tabernacle scene reminds me that the Lamb also represents peace. In God's kingdom, "the wolf and the lamb shall pasture together" on God's holy mountain.[18] Fittingly, the *Agnus Dei* that we pray at Mass concludes "Lamb of God, you take away the sins of the world, grant us peace."

---

[16] Isa 53:7, "Though harshly treated, he submitted and did not open his mouth; Like a lamb led to slaughter or a sheep silent before shearers, he did not open his mouth."

[17] Luke 10:3.

[18] Isa 65:25.

Photograph 26—Sacred Heart Catholic Church, Colorado Springs, CO. Used with permission.

Lamb imagery culminates in Revelation, where those who are saved from tribulation wash their robes clean in the blood of the

Lamb.[19] They are made innocent and pure, represented by the white of their robes. They stand before God's throne and worship Him.[20] As Revelation promises, "the Lamb who is in the center of the throne will shepherd them and lead them to springs of life-giving water and God will wipe away every tear from their eyes."[21] The lamb with a flag signifies the resurrection of Jesus and Christ's victory over death. The Book of Revelation portrays the lamb victorious over death, sitting on his throne, and leading those "who came out of the great tribulation."

Photograph 27—St. Patrick Catholic Church, Casper, WY.
Used with permission.

---

[19] Rev 7:14.
[20] Rev 7:15.
[21] Rev 7:17.

The victorious Lamb appears on a rectangular tabernacle at Saint Patrick Catholic Church in Casper, Wyoming. This tabernacle combines the themes of sacrifice and resurrection side by side. The left half of the tabernacle depicts the pelican, discussed earlier, and the right shows a lamb holding a staff aloft with a banner. The pelican motif also appears on the base of the pedestal supporting the tabernacle. The style here is bold and geometric with detailed sculpting of the pelican and lamb in silver on a golden tabernacle. Each motif is surrounded by four gold squares set with red gems and by a rectangular band of silver above and below it. The effect is to form a solid large cross from the empty space between the two motifs. Above that cross, the roof of the tabernacle rises slightly to a point that holds a small globe out of which rises a slender golden cross. This tabernacle not only combines sacrifice and resurrection but also strength and delicacy.

Another tabernacle boldly and colorfully depicts the triumphant Lamb of God in conjunction with the cross. In Englewood, Ohio, the tabernacle in the Blessed Sacrament Chapel at Saint Paul Catholic Church depicts the lamb with a halo behind its raised head. The lamb carries a staff topped with a cross bearing a banner with a red cross, representing sacrifice, on a field of white, representing purity. Red appears again in abstract squares behind the lamb. Golden beams of light, representing divinity, radiate forth from the tabernacle.

Chapter Five: Sacrifice 75

Photograph 28—Blessed Sacrament Chapel, St. Paul Catholic Church, Englewood, OH. Used with permission.

Prayer/Devotion

Lord, you are the Lamb of God sacrificed for our sins to bring us to everlasting life. You call us to imitate you, to go out as lambs among wolves, to be meek and mild yet prudent and wise. Stay with us, dear Lamb of God, and make us like you. Dwell in our souls and grant us peace in moments of fear, love in place of violence, surrendering all to the will of the Father. Lead us home to you, who are both the Lamb and the Good Shepherd who never abandons the least of His flock. Amen.

CHAPTER SIX

Jesus

Now that we've looked at the purpose-related themes of nourishment and sacrifice, let's examine typical portrayals in tabernacle art of Jesus who dwells within. We'll start with the name of Jesus, move to scenes from His life on Earth, and then look at Jesus as the Good Shepherd and the Light of the World. I'll conclude the chapter with the Anchor, symbolizing Jesus Our Hope. Not surprisingly, tabernacles bear images of Christ because He dwells within them. All of these may inspire your conversation with Him as you rest in His Presence.

Christograms

Many tabernacles incorporate the name of Jesus Christ in a monogram, called a Christogram. Sometimes, a Christogram is the primary decoration. For instance, the Chi Rho is a Christian symbol formed from the first two letters of Christ in Greek: X and P.

In Wyoming Catholic College's chapel in Lander, Wyoming, a smooth golden cylindrical tabernacle displays a large Chi Rho. On top of the tabernacle is a simple Celtic cross. This type of cross uses a circle at the center to express eternity and the endless love of God.[1]

---

[1] Some attribute the Celtic Cross to Saint Patrick who added the circle, previously a symbol of the sun god or moon goddess, to evangelize the pagan kings of Ireland. He may have intended it to represent God's light and life. Many Christians now view it as a symbol of the everlasting love of

Within this small chapel in Wyoming, light bounces off the tabernacle's smooth surface, giving it the appearance of molten gold out of which the name of Jesus emerges, a fitting container for the treasure it holds.

Photograph 29—Wyoming Catholic College Chapel, Lander, WY. Used with permission.

God and the eternal hope of salvation through Jesus Christ. Bernock, Danielle, "The Celtic Cross – Its Origin and Meaning," *Christianity.com*, (July 5, 2019), https://www.christianity.com/church/what-is-the-celtic-cross-its-origin-and-meaning.html#google_vignette.

Chapter Six: Jesus

More frequently, the Chi Rho appears as one of several design elements on a tabernacle. For example, a colorful modern tabernacle at Saint Maximilian Kolbe Church in Port Charlotte, Florida, places the Chi Rho on a host suspended over a chalice, surrounded by blades of wheat and bunches of grapes. The Chi Rho clearly identifies the host as Jesus. Behind it, a series of concentric circles evokes the light of the sun. On top of the tabernacle a slender gold cross repeats the cross pattern outside the Chi Rho on the tabernacle door.

Another symbol based on the letters of the Greek alphabet uses the alpha and omega, the first and last letters. Together, they signify the comprehensive nature of God. Both the Father and the Son refer to themselves as the Alpha and the Omega. The Book of Revelation proclaims that God is the first and the last, the beginning and the end.[2] This everlasting unending nature of God reminds us that God is outside of time. We experience this ourselves at every Mass when consecration of the Eucharist transports us to Calvary to be present at the one, perfect sacrifice of Jesus.

One with the Father and Holy Spirit, Jesus too is both the beginning and the end.[3] Transported to a heavenly realm by an angel, the author of Revelation sees "one like a son of man" who touches him and says, "Do not be afraid. I am the first and the last, the one who lives. Once I was dead, but now I am alive forever and ever. I hold the keys to death and the netherworld."[4] Jesus as the bridegroom of

---

[2] Rev. 1:8.
[3] Rev. 1:17-18; Rev 22:13.
[4] Rev. 1:13, 17-18.

the heavenly city, the new Jerusalem, His Church, proclaims, "I [am] the Alpha and the Omega, the beginning and the end."[5]

Photograph 30—St. Maximilian Kolbe Catholic Church, Port Charlotte, FL. Used with permission.

---

[5] Rev. 22:13 and 16 (Jesus sent his angel to deliver the message, "I am the Alpha and the Omega, the first and the last, the beginning and the end").

Chapter Six: Jesus

We also see Jesus, the Word of God, in the beginning, creating all things, in the Gospel of John.[6] The ancient Jewish understanding of God reflected the concept of the beginning and the end.[7] The Hebrew word for truth (*emeth*) begins with the first and ends with the last letters of the Hebrew alphabet: aleph (in Greek, *alpha*) and thaw (in Greek, *omega*).[8] Thus, the term "the Alpha and Omega" in signifying the Almighty also denotes Jesus, who is the Truth. As one scholar explains, the aleph indicates there was no one before God from whom God could have received "the fullness of truth. The Thaw . . . signifies that God is the last of all things. There will be no one after Him to whom He could bequeath [truth]. Thus *Emeth* . . . express[es] that in God truth dwells absolutely . . ."[9] As you come across tabernacles with an alpha and omega, contemplate how Jesus's preaching in the Gospels that He and God are one finds its roots in history, like so many of God's revelations.

At the Nativity of the Blessed Virgin Cathedral in Biloxi, Mississippi, a large alpha and omega prominently decorate the front of the tabernacle. Wheat and grapes surround them, while angels worship singing the Sanctus that stretches the length of the tabernacle just under its roof. The Holy Spirit in the form of a dove descends toward

---

[6] John 1:2.

[7] Kosloski, Philip. "What do the Alpha and Omega represent in Christian art?" *Aleteia* (May 29, 2017), https://aleteia.org/2017/05/29/what-do-the-alpha-and-omega-represent-in-christian-art.

[8] Van den Biesen, Christian. "Alpha and Omega." *The Catholic Encyclopedia*. Vol. 1. New York: Robert Appleton Company, 1907, http://www.newadvent.org/cathen/01332b.htm.

[9] *Id.*

the alpha and omega, much as the Spirit descended upon Jesus like a dove at His Baptism.[10]

Photograph 31—Nativity of the Blessed Virgin Mary Cathedral, Biloxi, MS. Used with permission.

---

[10] See Matt 3:16.

Chapter Six: Jesus

Other Christograms commonly used in tabernacle design are the IX and the IHS. The IX combines the first letter I for Iota of the name Jesus (*Iesous*) in Greek with X or Chi for *Christos* (Christ). Sometimes the IX appears inside a circle signifying the eternal nature of Jesus Christ. The I and X may be overlaid on top of one another to form one symbol.

IHS is a contraction of the name of Jesus. They are the first three letters of Jesus's name in Greek. A variation of this Christogram is IH. It too stands for the name of Jesus based on the Greek letters.

Interestingly, there are a variety of alternative explanations for the meaning of IHS. Many believe that the IHS came to be used because in Latin they are the first letters of the three words Jesus the Savior of Mankind: *Iesus* (Jesus) *Hominum* (of humankind) *Salvator* (Savior). Yet another theory posits that they come from the motto the Roman Emperor Constantine adopted after the battle that solidified his control. The night before battle, Constantine looked at the sky and saw a cross in a vision. At the same moment, he heard the words, "In this sign, you shall conquer" or, in Latin, "*In Hoc Signo Vinces.*" Reportedly, he directed his soldiers to paint the sign of the cross on their shields before he fought and won the battle.[11]

Both Saint Bernadine and Saint Ignatius of Loyola spread use of the IHS. As a symbol of the Holy Name of Jesus, Saint Bernadine

---

[11] Darcy, Peter. "What Does the IHS Symbol Really Mean?" *Catholic Stand*, Sept. 14, 2022, https://catholicstand.com/what-does-the-ihs-symbol-really-mean.

encouraged Christians to write it on their doorways.[12] Later, Saint Ignatius adopted IHS as the motto of his newly founded order, the Society of Jesus.[13]

Photograph 32—St. Francis de Solano Catholic Church, Sonoma, CA. Used with permission.

---

[12] Kosloski, Philip. "St. Bernardine of Siena's prayer to the Holy Name of Jesus," *Aleteia* (Jan. 14, 2019), https://aleteia.org/2019/01/14/st-bernardine-of-sienas-prayer-to-the-holy-name-of-jesus.

[13] Maere, R. "IHS," *The Catholic Encyclopedia*, New York: Robert Appleton Company, 1910, https://www.newadvent.org/cathen/07649a.htm#:~:text=A.

At Saint Francis de Solano Catholic Church in Sonoma, California, the IHS appears behind the cross on the front of the tabernacle. The linens under the tabernacle repeat the IHS interspersed with embroidered bunches of grapes.

All these Christograms, like other symbols described in this book, stand for things we cannot capture in words, yet they themselves are incomplete. A symbol represents something but is not the thing itself. The Eucharist is not a symbol of Christ; it is Christ. The use of symbols in tabernacles reminds us of the limits of our understanding, but also of the joy we will have in pondering God, in being with Him in eternity where we will see Him clearly, not through a clouded mirror.[14] There, without a veil or tabernacle, we will be present face to face with our Lord, to gaze upon His glory and participate fully in relationship with Him. Let us spend time before Jesus now in the tabernacle as we pray to be united with Him fully in the future.

Prayer/Devotion

As you pray before a tabernacle with a Christogram, ponder what symbols could mean using your own language about your relationship with Christ. Perhaps IHS might stand for "In His Service" or IH "In Him"? Can IHS express the reality that you are "In His Sight" always? Does IH call you to recognize the True Presence of

---

[14] *See* 1 Cor 13:12, "Now we see a dim reflection, as if we were looking into a mirror, but then we shall see clearly. Now I know only a part, but then I will know fully, as God has known me."

Christ by summarizing "I'm Here"? You might even take a suggestion from autocorrect which persistently changes IHS to HIS.

Whisper the name of Jesus to Him softly and lovingly. Recall Jesus means "God saves."

Pray the "Golden Arrow" prayer in reparation for misuse of the name of the Jesus: "May the most holy, most sacred, most adorable, most mysterious and unutterable Name of God be always praised, blessed, loved, adored and glorified in heaven, on earth, and under the earth, by all the creatures of God, and by the Sacred Heart of our Lord Jesus Christ in the most Holy Sacrament of the altar."[15]

Meditate upon this reflection from Bishop Michael F. Burbidge:

> Saint Bernardine of Siena promoted devotion to the Holy Name of Jesus.
> May we never say the name of Jesus in moments of frustration or anger.
> Instead, may we only invoke the holy name of Jesus in *prayer, praise and thanksgiving* with all due respect and reverence.[16]

Recite Saint Bernardine's Prayer to the Holy Name of Jesus:

---

[15] "The Golden Arrow," *Our Catholic Prayers*, https://www.our-catholicprayers.com/golden-arrow.html.

[16] Burbidge, Most Reverend Michael F. *33 Spiritual Reflections for Daily Living* (Diocese of Arlington), https://www.arlingtondiocese.org/catechetical-resources/catechetical-messages-from-most-rev--michael-f--burbidge/.

Jesus, Name full of glory, grace, love and strength! You are the refuge of those who repent, our banner of warfare in this life, the medicine of souls, the comfort of those who mourn, the delight of those who believe, the light of those who preach the true faith, the wages of those who toil, the healing of the sick. To you our devotion aspires; by you our prayers are received; we delight in contemplating you. O Name of Jesus, you are the glory of all the saints for eternity. Amen.[17]

Finally, the Litany of the Holy Name of Jesus introduces us to the many names and titles of Jesus as we ask for His mercy and beg Him to save His people. You can find it on the USCCB website.[18] Is there a particular name or title of Jesus that you'd like to ask Him about as you sit by His side in the tabernacle?

Life of Jesus Christ

Themes from the life of Jesus Christ regularly decorate tabernacles and provide inspiration for reflection and prayer. Depictions of Jesus as an infant or child remind us that He made Himself vulnerable by becoming one of us in His humanity, so that we might be saved. Scenes from Jesus's life on Earth encourage us to read Scripture and reflect on the meaning of the particular event in context. Portrayals of the Last Supper, the Garden of Gethsemane, and the

---

[17] Kosloski, *supra* note 12.
[18] USCCB, "Litany of the Holy Name of Jesus," https://www.usccb.org/prayers/litany-holy-name-jesus.

crucifixion focus on Jesus's sacrifice. Some of these we've already examined in other chapters, but here I'd like to share a few more of the many beautiful examples I've found in my travels.

Photograph 33—Mission Basilica San Juan Capistrano, San Juan Capistrano, CA. Used with permission.

Chapter Six: Jesus 89

The tabernacle at the national shrine Mission Basilica San Juan Capistrano in California shows us the shepherds adoring the Infant Jesus in the stable. Mary holds Jesus and Joseph stands close by, watching over them. One shepherd kneels with outstretched arms, reaching toward Jesus. The other stands holding a lamb, signifying Jesus. We too can turn to Mary as our mother and ask Saint Joseph, guardian of the church, to intercede for our protection. We can worship the baby with the shepherds, acknowledging how remarkable it is that God should come to us as an infant totally dependent upon his parents.

Photograph 34—Arnold Hall Conference Center Chapel, Pembroke, MA. Used with permission.

Another delightful image appears on the tabernacle door at Arnold Hall Conference Center's chapel in Pembroke, Massachusetts. The young child Jesus walks between Mary and Joseph, holding their hands. I wonder if the child Jesus, like my children, would beg to be lifted up off the ground and swung, secure in Mary and Joseph's grip. I think of His humility in allowing Himself to be a child, to be taught by Mary and Joseph as he grew into a man. This tabernacle reminds me that we are children of God and that to be childlike is a gift. We too can go to Mary and Joseph and be supported in our walk of faith.

Photograph 35—Arnold Hall Conference Center Chapel, Pembroke, MA. Used with permission.

Chapter Six: Jesus 91

In addition to the charming portrait of Jesus as a child, the tabernacle depicts the Trinity. God the Father extends His arms over the Holy Family. God the Holy Spirit connects Jesus and the Father, making literal the bond of love between them that is the Holy Spirit. The archangels Michael and Raphael flank the door between columns that evoke a classical temple. The cross rests atop this tabernacle, reminding us of what the Holy Child was born to do for us.

While many tabernacles display crosses or crucifixes, discussed above, some depict the scenes of Christ's passion. Jesus's face beneath the crown of thorns sometimes adorns tabernacles, as in these two examples from the Southwest. The elaborate altar at Mission San Antonio de Padua in Jolon, California, presents the tabernacle in a traditional Spanish-style reredos, while the one in Saint John Neumann Church in Yuma, Arizona, is less elaborate. Whether by painted wood or through sculpted metal, both convey the sorrowful agony of the beloved Face of Jesus.

Photograph 36— Mission San Antonio de Padua, Jolon, CA.
Used with permission.

Photograph 37— Saint John Neumann Catholic Church, Yuma, AZ. Used with permission.

Scenes of the crucifixion usually depict the Virgin Mary and Saint John at the foot of the cross, and sometimes Saint Mary Magdalene. Such images let us see the cost of the salvation Jesus won for us as we contemplate His Real Presence with us in the Eucharist. In this tabernacle from the Cathedral of Saint Mary in Colorado Springs, Colorado, the apostle John and Mother Mary stand at the foot of the cross accompanying Jesus in the last of his passion. We can accompany Him, too, by offering our sufferings with His. By placing our sorrows and sacrifices on the altar at Mass, we lay them gently at the foot of the cross.

Chapter Six: Jesus

Photograph 38—St. Mary's Cathedral, Colorado Springs, CO. Used with permission.

Finally, you may discover tabernacle art showing the Resurrection or Ascension of Christ, completing His physical time on Earth until He returns at the end of time. On the tabernacle at Sacred Heart Catholic Church in Caro, Michigan, the Resurrected Christ stands between the empty tomb and the three empty crosses at Golgotha. Until Christ returns, His sacramental presence reminds us all of His humanity and divinity and witnesses to His love. He never leaves us orphans but is always present. Lay your heart down before Him at a tabernacle. He fills it with His love.

*Photograph 39—Sacred Heart Catholic Church, Caro, MI.
Used with permission.*

Prayer/Devotion

Reflect upon a scene from the life of Jesus. Place yourself mentally in the scene. What would you do or say? What is He saying to you?

Pray the Rosary, contemplating scenes from the life of Jesus and Mary. You may have a favorite mystery that relates to the tabernacle theme before you, such as, for instance, the Third Joyful Mystery (the Nativity) as depicted above (see

Chapter Six: Jesus

photograph 33) on the tabernacle from San Juan Capistrano. Like the magi and shepherds at the manger in Bethlehem, you come to kneel before Jesus, to adore and worship Him. [19]

Another source of reflection on Jesus's passion, death, and resurrection may be found in the Stations of the Cross devotion. Churches often have booklets available for this devotion and it is readily available online. The Stations of the Cross most often is prayed during Fridays in Lent but provides great spiritual value at any time.

The Good Shepherd

In his great love for us, Jesus leads us home to Heaven as the Good Shepherd. While the Lamb, discussed above, is a symbol of Jesus as sacrifice and victory over death, the Good Shepherd imagery is distinct. It focuses on seeking and finding the lost sheep, and guiding us, even carrying us, home to lush green pastures, to the safety of the flock led by Jesus as shepherd.

---

[19]Many guides exist for praying the Rosary, with varying focus and emphasis, but all with the same prayers. One of these may appeal to you in particular: *Praying the Holy Rosary with Saint Josemaria*, available on Amazon and from the Saint Josemaria Institute at https://stjosemaria.org/product/praying-the-holy-rosary-with-st-josemaria; *A Scriptural Rosary for the Family*, available from the Knights of Columbus at https://kofc.org/en/resources/faith-in-action-programs/faith/rosary-program/319-scriptural-rosary.pdf; USCCB, *Rosaries*, available at https://www.usccb.org/prayer-and-worship/prayers-and-devotions/rosaries.

This contrasts with, but does not contradict, the motif of Jesus as the lamb who is sacrificed to save us from our sins. "To be a Christian is to expect things to turn around. God reverses things; a slaughtered sheep becomes our shepherd. The lamb who was slaughtered on Good Friday has actually become seated victoriously on the throne. The suffering lamb has actually become the Good Shepherd of the whole world."[20]

Early depictions of the Good Shepherd carrying a lamb on His shoulders date to the first century. In the artwork of the catacombs, the lamb represented the soul of the deceased being carried by Christ home to Heaven, accompanied by other lambs as the saints.[21]

Scripture contains many references to the shepherd. For instance, Isaiah prophesies the coming of the Messiah as a shepherd: "Like a shepherd He feeds his flock; in his arms he gathers the lambs, Carrying them in his bosom, leading the ewes with care."[22] And, perhaps the most recognized psalm is that of the Good Shepherd, specifically these oft-cited lines: "The Lord is my shepherd; there is nothing I lack. In green pastures he makes me lie down; to still waters he leads me; he restores my soul. He guides me along right paths for the sake of his name."[23]

---

[20] Candler, Very Rev. Sam, "Homily on the Fourth Sunday of Easter: The Shepherd is a Lamb," Website of the Cathedral of Saint Philip, Atlanta, Georgia (April 30, 2023), https://www.cathedralatl.org/sermons/the-shepherd-is-a-lamb.

[21] Hassett, Maurice. "The Lamb (in Early Christian Symbolism)." *The Catholic Encyclopedia*. Vol. 8. New York: Robert Appleton Company, 1910. 18 Aug. 2023 <http://www.newadvent.org/cathen/08755b.htm>.

[22] Isa 40:11.

[23] Ps 23:1-3.

The Good Shepherd heals us through His abundant love and care, much as the Lamb heals the wounds and sufferings of sin through His sacrifice. Like Jesus in the Eucharist, the Good Shepherd remains with us: "Even though I walk through the valley of the shadow of death, I will fear no evil, for you are with me; your rod and your staff comfort me." [24]

A painting on the door of the golden tabernacle at Mission Basilica San Buenaventura in Ventura, California, depicts Jesus as the Good Shepherd. Clothed in blue, with a lamb slung around His shoulders, Jesus walks barefoot on the dirt. One hand gently clasps the lamb's tiny legs, and the other firmly holds the shepherd's staff. Dark clouds surround Jesus and the lamb, but part around His head to reveal a soft nimbus of light.

Jesus, our Light and our shepherd, carry us through the storms!

Prayer/Devotion

Recite Psalm 23, imagining yourself being carried by Jesus.

Ponder this reflection from Bishop Michael F. Burbidge:

> Jesus says: "I am the good shepherd and I know mine and mine know me." Reflect on that beautiful reality: *Jesus knows you by name!* Strive to know him more deeply by listening to his voice in prayer, the Good Shepherd who promises to lead, guide and protect you. [25]

---

[24] Ps 23:1-4.

[25] Burbidge, *supra* note 16 (emphasis in original).

Photograph 40—Mission Basilica San Buenaventura, Ventura, CA. Used with permission.

You may enjoy a lovely prayer for a restful night's sleep, based on Psalm 23. It reads in part: "In my sleep, lead me beside quiet waters. Keep me from evil, that I may walk in righteousness by Your power and provision. Let no evil enter my mind tonight, and guard

Chapter Six: Jesus

me against fearful or anxious thoughts. You are my Shepherd every hour of the day . . . [and] night."[26]

For further reflections and meditation on the Good Shepherd, see the readings and commentary from the Fourth Sunday of Easter at Catholicculture.org (April 30, 2023).[27]

Light of the World

Tabernacles that depict light reflect how all things came to be through Jesus, the Word of God. He brought life to the world, and this life was "the light of the human race."[28] The tabernacle lamp, usually a red or white candle, reminds us that "the light shines in the darkness and the darkness has not overcome it."[29] Light thus signifies the presence of God, an apt motif for a tabernacle.

More than the life created in the beginning, Jesus brings us life in the Blessed Sacrament. There in the tabernacle, light shines forth illuminating, purifying, healing the darkest corners of our souls. We receive eternal life through Jesus's sacrifice, and through the grace of Communion we experience that life and light in unity with Jesus and all others receiving Communion.

When I arrived at my latest camp-hosting volunteer gig at Sebago Lake State Park in Casco, Maine, in April 2023, I was delighted

---

[26] 3 Scriptures to Pray Every Evening, *Scripture Lullabies* (Nov 12, 2020), https://scripture-lullabies.com/3-scriptures-to-pray-every-evening. Used with permission.

[27] https://www.catholicculture.org/culture/liturgicalyear/calendar/day.cfm?date=2023-04-30.

[28] John 1:3.

[29] John 1:5.

to find daily Mass nearby. Our Lady of Perpetual Help of Saint Anthony's Parish in the Diocese of Portland (Maine) is just off Roosevelt Trail (Rt. 302), the main road around the northern and western part of Sebago Lake. The modest church attracts many summer visitors as well as local residents. Parishioners and the pastor, Father Lou Phillips, made this pilgrim feel very welcome. Bible studies, book clubs, opportunities to volunteer, and coffee after Mass helped me feel at home in this community. The parish has a very active social-justice ministry, including prison ministry and feeding the needy in the community with other area churches. The Knights of Columbus sponsor many parish and charitable events as well. This outreach follows Jesus in bringing His light to the world around us.

Fittingly, the tabernacle at Our Lady of Perpetual Help evokes Jesus as the Light of the World. The small silver tabernacle portrays stylized geometric rays that spread out from an abstract circular sun in the center. The vertical lines on the altar cloths beneath the tabernacle suggest streams of running water spilling over from His dwelling.

This tabernacle also reminds me of the rays of Divine Mercy issuing from Jesus's heart in Sister Faustina's visions. The love of the Son is so strong it radiates from His Heart to ours. Our Eucharistic Lord fills us with His grace so that we can love as He loves. Light shines forth as we go forth from the Mass to bring Christ's light to the world.

Chapter Six: Jesus 101

*Photograph 41—Our Lady of Perpetual Help, Windham, ME.
Used with permission.*

The simplicity of the tabernacle at Our Lady of Perpetual Help and its humble setting also appeal to me. Even in unexpected places, not well known beyond the local community, one finds fountains of grace and beauty. Abstract art can lead to contemplation as well as pictorial sculpture can.

Photograph 42—Saint Luke Catholic Church, Ogallala, NE. Used with permission.

Chapter Six: Jesus

Far from Maine, while following the Oregon Trail with fellow Airstreamers,[30] I came across a simple yet rich tabernacle at Saint Luke Catholic Church in Ogallala, Nebraska. The gold of the door complements the sienna tones of the marble surrounding it. The art depicts a chalice holding a host with the IHS Christogram. From the host, strong beams of light spread outward. Waves of water or billowing clouds representing the Holy Spirit swirl about the bottom and sides of the chalice. The radiating beams of light that touch the clouds disappear into them.

This makes me think of the *epiclesis* during Mass. During the epiclesis, the priest prays with his hands outstretched over the chalice and paten that God the Father will send down the Holy Spirit to transform and sanctify the offerings of bread and wine: "Make holy, therefore, these gifts, we pray, by sending down your Spirit upon them like the dewfall, so that they may become for us the Body and Blood of our Lord Jesus Christ."[31]

Very similar artwork decorates the tabernacle at Saint Francis of Assisi Catholic Church in La Quinta, California. There, the chalice rests on waves of water. The rounded curve of the tabernacle door echoes the marble arch above it. This white marble tabernacle with a golden door resembles a Romanesque temple or church.[32] Here

---

[30] Airstreamers are people who travel and camp in recreational vehicles made by Airstream. For several years, I made my movable home in an iconic Airstream travel trailer, amusingly called a "Flying Cloud." Currently, I travel in an Airstream Rangeline Class B camper van.

[31] Eucharistic Prayer II, Order of Mass.

[32] *See* Chapter Eight for further discussion of tabernacles depicting church architecture.

again the predominant theme is Jesus in His Real Presence (the Host and Precious Blood) as the Light of the World, embodied by rays of light.

Photograph 43—St. Francis of Assisi Catholic Church, La Quinta, CA. Used with permission.

Finally, the wall tabernacle at Saint Philip Catholic Church in Franklin, Tennessee, fairly explodes with rays of light and stars. While light is the primary theme of this tabernacle, it contains many other symbols discussed in other sections of this book. The circular

Chapter Six: Jesus   105

center from which rays spread forth contains a host and chalice, surrounded by grapes and grain below it and thorns and stars above it.[33] This modern depiction again shows the variety with which love of Our Eucharistic Lord manifests itself in art.

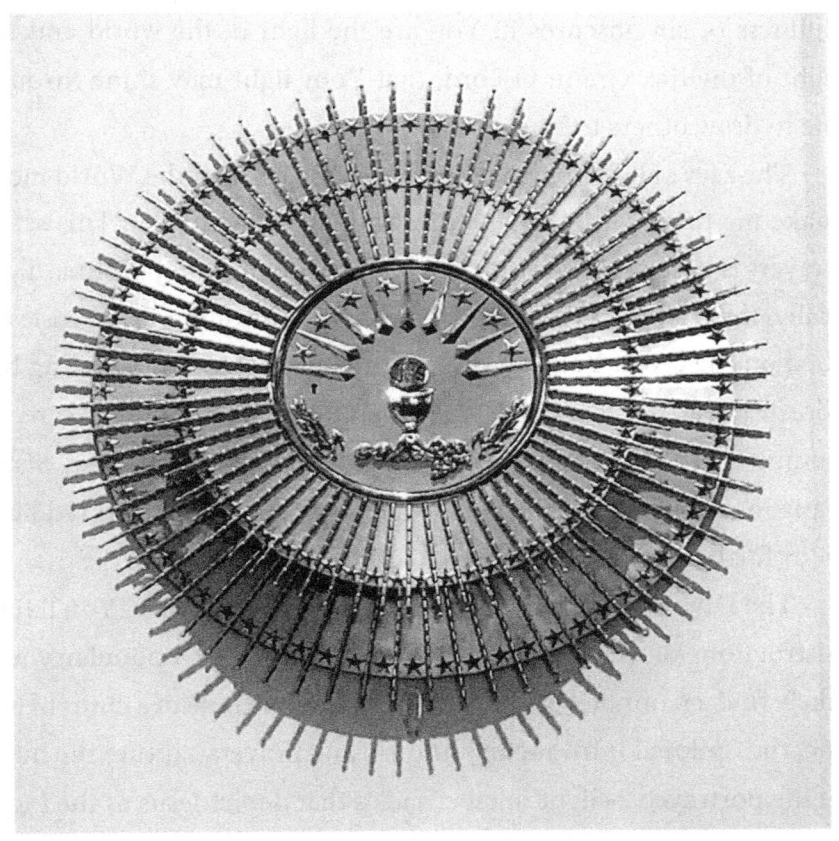

Photograph 44—St. Philip Catholic Church, Franklin, TN. Used with permission.

---

[33] *See* Chapter Four (Nourishment, sections discussing images of the Blessed Sacrament and Grapes and Grain); Chapter Six (Jesus, section discussing images of the crucifixion).

Prayer/Devotion

Lord Jesus, enlighten our minds and hearts. Open our eyes to see You truly present here with us and in us. Help us to see Your light in all things, in creation, in other people, even where darkness and dullness of sin obscures it. You are the light of the world and the light of my life. Grant, O Lord, that Your light may shine through me to draw others to You.

The rays of light in tabernacles with the Light of the World motif make me think of the Divine Mercy image and chaplet. This set of prayers is based on revelations of Jesus made to Saint Faustina. Typically, the chaplet is prayed at 3 p.m., the hour of mercy when Jesus died on the cross. You can pray it anytime, however, including before Jesus at the tabernacle. You may have seen a prayer card or painting of the Divine Mercy image that Jesus instructed Sister Faustina to have made. In this image, beams of white and red light pour forth from Jesus's heart as a fountain of mercy for us.

The Divine Mercy chaplet is prayed on rosary beads. You'll find instructions on how to pray it online,[34] but it is so popular you'll likely find a pamphlet or prayer card in the vestibule of a church. For me, the optional introductory and closing prayers capture the burst of life portrayed as light in tabernacles that depict Jesus as the Light of the World. He gives us life in Him, through His sacrifice and His mercy. The introductory prayer reads:

---

[34] *See* The Divine Mercy, "How to Recite the Chaplet," https://www.thedivinemercy.org/message/devotions/pray-the-chaplet.

You expired, Jesus, but the source of life gushed forth for souls, and the ocean of mercy opened up for the whole world.

O Fount of Life, unfathomable Divine Mercy, envelop the whole world and empty Yourself out upon us.

O Blood and Water, which gushed forth from the Heart of Jesus as a fountain of Mercy for us, I trust in You!

The chaplet's optional closing prayer echoes the call of Jesus to be light to the world [35] — a light of mercy — by asking that God's mercy work within us to allow us to submit ourselves confidently to His will:

Eternal God, in whom mercy is endless and the treasury of compassion inexhaustible, look kindly upon us and increase Your mercy in us, that in difficult moments we might not despair nor become despondent, but with great confidence submit ourselves to Your holy will, which is Love and Mercy itself. [36]

The Anchor

In ancient times anchors symbolized security based on their importance to navigation. An anchor tethers a ship in one location. By

---

[35] *See* Matt. 5:14-16, "You are the light of the world. . . . Your light must shine before others, that they may see your good deeds and glorify your Heavenly Father."

[36] USCCB, *How to Pray the Chaplet of Divine Mercy*, https://www.usccb.org/prayers/how-pray-chaplet-divine-mercy.

mooring the ship, the anchor prevents it from being swept away by wind and waves.

Scripture says hope is set before us "as an anchor of the soul, sure and firm."[37] Christians adopted the anchor symbol to mean hope, specifically that Christ is the hope of all who believe in Him.[38] When combined with a cross or crucifix they refer to the work of Christians to bring hope to the world.[39] This remains the mission of every Christian: to proclaim "God is with us. This is the message of hope that we want to shout from the rooftops. . ."[40]

Early Christians facing persecution also used the anchor as a disguised symbol of the cross and the promise of salvation. The Catholic Encyclopedia elaborates "One of the most remarkable of these disguised crosses, from the cemetery of St. Domitilla, consists of an anchor placed upright, the transverse bar appearing just beneath the ring. To complete the symbol, two fishes are represented with the points of the curved branches in their mouths. A real cross, standing on a sort of pedestal to the right of this, is sufficient indication that

---

[37] Heb 6:19-20.

[38] *Catholic Encyclopedia*, "Anchors symbolize hope," https:/newadvent.org/cathen/01462a.htm.

[39] *Id.*

[40] Burbidge, Most Reverend Michael F. Pastoral Letter of Most Reverend Michael F. Burbidge, Bishop of Arlington. In Tongues All Can Hear: Communicating the Hope of Christ in Times of Trial (Sept. 15, 2020), https://www.arlingtondiocese.org/in-tongues-all-can-hear.

the author of the figures intended a symbolic cross in this instance."[41] The fish represented Christ on the cross of the anchor. By the fourth century, this use of the anchor as a symbol of crucifixion disappeared.[42]

The anchor remains a symbol of Christ, our hope and security.[43] According to Catholic tradition, the Roman Emperor Trajan had Pope Saint Clement murdered by tying him to an anchor thrown into the sea. For this reason, some refer to an anchor cross as Saint Clement's cross.[44] Although Pope Saint Clement died following the anchor to the depths, he lives now in Christ whom he followed in trust and hope to everlasting life.

At Saint Malachy Catholic Church in Rantoul, Illinois, the tabernacle's simple, streamlined anchor recalls Jesus as our strength and hope. A subtle Chi Rho marks the right top beam of the bold anchor. A circle behind the top of the anchor forms a St. Clement's cross. Beams of light radiate from the circle to the edges of the tabernacle door. At the top and bottom of this cylindrical tabernacle, regular vertical indentations suggest a widow's walk or the railing of a ship. Above, a dove descends onto the tabernacle from its highest point.

---

[41] Hassett, Maurice. "The Anchor (as Symbol)." *The Catholic Encyclopedia*. Vol. 1. New York: Robert Appleton Company, 1907, http://www.newadvent.org/cathen/01462a.htm.

[42] *Id.*

[43] "Why are there anchors in Christian art?" *Aleteia* (June 10, 2017), https://aleteia.org/2017/06/10/why-are-there-anchors-in-christian-art.

[44] "Pope Clement I," *New World Encyclopedia*, https://www.newworldencyclopedia.org/entry/Pope_Clement_I.

*Photograph 45—St. Malachy Catholic Church, Rantoul, IL.
Used with permission.*

A more delicate and ornate anchor tabernacle rests at Mission Soledad in Soledad, California. Fanciful metalwork traces thin grape vines with detailed leaves and bunches of grapes in filigree waves around the edges of the tabernacle. By contrast, strong, bold curves of flat hammered metal form an anchor on the tabernacle door. This anchor incorporates an alpha and omega within its lines. Thus, the tabernacle draws from multiple symbols to communicate the eternal steadfastness of God. We also find strength within the fanciful waves formed by grapevines as we adore the Body and Blood made present within the tabernacle.

Chapter Six: Jesus 111

Photograph 46—Mission Soledad Catholic Chapel, Soledad, CA. Used with permission.

For me, an anchor means something that keeps me tethered. Prayer in this sense anchors me. When I fail to pray regularly, I wander and become adrift, caught up in the currents of everyday tasks or the tumult of passing storms. My hope is in Christ, the anchor of my soul. In still waters or rough, in gales and gusts, He keeps me safe and secure in His love. He is the foundation of my hope, and I trust in His promise of life with Him forever.

Prayer/Devotion

As you sit with the Lord in His sacramental presence, ponder the meaning of the anchor for you. You may wish to read the following Scripture passages as you reflect upon how Christ anchors you. Note that the first quote which speaks of hope as an anchor does so in the context of hope entering into the tabernacle, "the inner shrine behind the curtain." How fitting then that an anchor should adorn the exterior of a tabernacle. There, the Blessed Sacrament resides as hope made real, as Love Incarnate, body and soul, humanity and divinity.

> "This we have as an anchor of the soul, sure and firm, which reaches into the interior behind the veil, where Jesus has entered on our behalf as forerunner, becoming high priest forever according to the order of Melchizedek."
>
> Hebrews 6:19-20.

> "Do not fear: I am with you; do not be anxious: I am your God. I will strengthen you, I will help you, I will uphold you with my victorious right hand."
>
> Isaiah 41:10.

> "The Lord is my light and my salvation; whom should I fear? The Lord is my life's refuge; of whom should I be afraid?"
>
> Psalm 27:1.

"My soul rests in God alone, from whom comes my salvation.... My soul, be at rest in God alone, from whom comes my hope. God alone is my rock and my salvation, my fortress; I shall not fall."

Psalm 62:2, 6-7.

CHAPTER SEVEN

Spirit

Now that we've looked at tabernacle art expressing themes of nourishment, sacrifice, and Jesus, let's turn to the Holy Spirit, the third person of the Trinity, and to angels, spiritual beings present at every Mass, worshipping Jesus in the consecrated host and wine. The Holy Spirit brings Jesus to us in the Eucharist, while the angels invite us to join them in praise and worship of God made present in the Tabernacle.

The Holy Spirit

Jesus did not leave us orphans, or leave us alone, when He ascended to the Father. Instead, He left so that the Third Person of the Trinity, the Holy Spirit, could descend to the disciples.[1] Of course, Jesus also remained with them, and remains with us, in the Blessed Sacrament. During the consecration of the host and wine, the priest calls upon the Holy Spirit. Likewise, we too can call upon the Holy Spirit in worshipping before the consecrated host in the tabernacle. Indeed, "the Holy Spirit inspires all prayer within the deep recesses of the human heart. ... the Catechism recommends that we invoke the Holy Spirit at the beginning and end of every occupation."[2] This can include our visits to the tabernacle.

---

[1] See John 16:7.
[2] Armenio, *supra* note 19, Chapter 1.

Not surprisingly, tabernacles containing the Real Presence of Jesus often incorporate symbols of the Holy Spirit in their design. We've already discussed the use of wind or clouds to depict the Spirit in conjunction with other symbols of Jesus and the Eucharist. Here, we'll look at tabernacle art in which the Holy Spirit is the dominant theme.

Photograph 47—Resurrection Catholic Church, Randolph, NJ. Used with permission.

Flames depicted on a tabernacle refer to the Holy Spirit, as this very literal example above from Resurrection Catholic Church in

Chapter Seven: Spirit

Randolph, New Jersey, illustrates. The entire tabernacle is a sculpture of a flame. The love between the Father and the Son bursts forth into fire, blazing into our hearts and igniting our faith.

Another point to ponder in viewing this tabernacle is that it also represents the burning bush where God appeared to Moses.[3] The holy ground beneath Moses' feet millennia ago is here, now, before every tabernacle in which Jesus Christ, the Second Person of the Holy Trinity, dwells in His Real Presence. We have the incredible gift of being able to see Him, touch Him, eat Him to become Christ-like, thanks to the Holy Spirit working through the priest to consecrate a simple wafer of bread and a cup of wine.

The symbolism of the Holy Spirit as fire is solidly grounded in Scripture. As Jesus relates parables to His disciples in the Gospel of Luke, He tells them, "I have come to set the earth on fire, and how I wish it were already blazing!"[4] Flames represent the Holy Spirit or God in other places in the Bible, such as the burning bush Moses encounters and the column of fire that accompanies the Israelites in the wilderness.[5] At Pentecost, the Holy Spirit descends upon the apostles and Mary in the form of flame.[6] (And it is the Holy Spirit that the priest invokes at Mass at the start of the transformation of the bread and wine into the Body and Blood of Jesus Christ.[7])

---

[3] Exod 3:2-5. I am grateful to Rev. John F. Tarantino, Pastor of Resurrection Parish, who suggested this interpretation when I requested permission to use my photograph of the tabernacle.

[4] Luke 12:49.

[5] Exod 3:2; Exod 13:21-22.

[6] Acts 2:1-4.

[7] *See* discussion of epiclesis in Chapter Six.

Just as light and flame are symbols of the Holy Spirit so are depictions of wind, clouds, and water.[8] Many tabernacles use these and other symbols of the Holy Spirit. Perhaps the most common image is a dove. At Jesus's baptism, the Holy Spirit appears as a dove who descends upon Jesus. As discussed earlier, early Christians literally placed the reserved Eucharist inside a metal figure of a dove suspended above the altar.[9] Over time, the dove holding the Eucharist was placed inside a fixed tower. Now, doves often decorate the altar and tabernacle.

Remarkably, the Bethany Chapel at the Archdiocese of Boston's Pastoral Center in Braintree, Massachusetts, unites past and present in its tabernacle. Fine chains attached to the ceiling of the chapel suspend a silver dove tabernacle directly above the altar. This replica of ancient dove tabernacles may be lowered to replenish or access the consecrated hosts it contains. I did not have the chance to observe this process in person as the presiding priest consecrated sufficient hosts for immediate needs at the Mass I attended there.

In addition to being a symbol of the Holy Spirit, doves can be a sign of peace, purity, and hope. Noah sent forth a dove to determine if it was safe for the ark to land, representing hope.[10] The image of

---

[8] CCC 694, 697. *See also* CCC 691: "The term "Spirit" translates the Hebrew word *ruah*, which, in its primary sense, means breath, air, wind. Jesus indeed uses the sensory image of the wind to suggest to Nicodemus the transcendent newness of him who is personally God's breath, the divine Spirit."

[9] *See* Barnes, Arthur. "Dove." The Catholic Encyclopedia. Vol. 5. New York: Robert Appleton Company, 1909. http://www.newadvent.org/cathen/05144b.htm.

[10] Gen 8:8-12.

Chapter Seven: Spirit   119

the dove returning to Noah with an olive branch in its mouth signifies peace. Twelve doves surrounding the cross stand for the twelve apostles.[11]

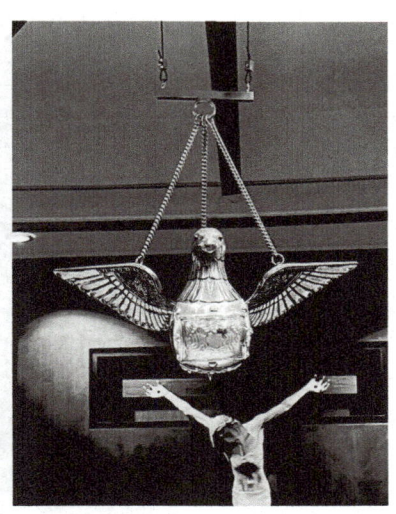

Photographs 48 and 49—Bethany Chapel, Archdiocese of Boston Pastoral Center, Braintree, MA. Used with permission.

Rays of light emanating from the dove may express a variety of different concepts based on the number of rays, such as, for example, the Trinity (three) or the fruits of the Holy Spirit (nine).[12]

---

[11] Dove, *supra* note 9.

[12] Van Sloun, Rev. Michael, "Different Portrayals of the Holy Spirit as a Dove," *The Catholic Spirit* (June 7, 2019), https://thecatholicspirit.com/commentary/hotdish/different-portrayals-of-the-holy-spirit-as-a-dove. The fruits of the Holy Spirt are love, joy, peace, patience, kindness, generosity, faithfulness, gentleness, and self-control. Gal.5:22-23.

Often, tabernacle art includes a dove on top of the tabernacle, representing the descent of the Holy Spirit, as witnessed at Jesus's baptism.[13]

Photograph 50—Shrine of St. Joseph, Stirling, NJ. Used with permission.

At the Shrine of Saint Joseph in Stirling, New Jersey, a dove dominates the carved wooden tabernacle, flanked by the hand of God and the cross of Jesus depicting all three persons of the Most Holy

---

[13] Matt 3:16.

Chapter Seven: Spirit

Trinity. Waves flow over the tabernacle, and rays of light spring up from it. This tabernacle, like others bearing symbols of the Holy Spirit, reminds us to engage that third person of the Trinity in our prayer.

Prayer/ Devotion:

The traditional prayer invoking the Holy Spirit is one of my favorites when I visit the tabernacle:

> Come, Holy Spirit,
> fill the hearts of your faithful
> and enkindle in them the fire of your love.
> Send forth your Spirit and they shall be created
> and You shall renew the face of the earth.
> O God, who has taught the hearts of the faithful
> by the light of the Holy Spirit,
> Grant that by the gift of the same Spirit
> we may be truly wise
> and ever rejoice in his consolation
> through Christ our Lord. Amen.

Saint Augustine provides an especially beautiful prayer for asking the Holy Spirit for help in becoming holy:

> Breathe in me, O Holy Spirit,
> that my thoughts may all be holy.
> Act in me, O Holy Spirit,
> that my work, too, may be holy.
> Draw my heart, O Holy Spirit,

that I love but what is holy.
Strengthen me, O Holy Spirit,
to defend all that is holy.
Guard me, then, O Holy Spirit,
that I always may be holy. Amen.

Angels

Angels are pure spirits created by God to worship, glorify, and serve Him.[14] They possess immense intellect and perfect freedom of will. Humans each receive a guardian angel to guide and protect them.[15] According to God's will, the angels pray for us, bear messages from God to us, and sometimes intervene in our lives. Scripture is replete with examples.[16]

At every Mass, we join in worship with the angels as they eternally worship God in heaven. Indeed, the words of the Gloria prayed at Mass recall the angels' proclamation of the birth of Christ: "Glory to God in the Highest and on earth peace to people of good will."[17]

In tabernacle art, angels may kneel in worship, bear the cup of salvation, reverently hold the host, or protect the tabernacle. They can be found around the altar, on the top of tabernacles, and in many

---

[14] *See* CCC 328-333.

[15] *See* Matt 18:10; CCC 336.

[16] *See, e.g.,* Luke 1:11-17 (angel informing Zechariah that he will have a son); Luke 1: 26-38 (the Annunciation); Gen 21:17 (saving Hagar and her child).

[17] For a detailed discussion of the Gloria, *see* Thiron, Rita, "The Roman Missal: The Gloria," *Faith, The Magazine of the Catholic Diocese of Lansing* (May 2011), https://faithmag.com/roman-missal-gloria. *See also* Luke 2:14.

Chapter Seven: Spirit

other glass and stone depictions throughout churches.[18] God Himself instructed Moses to make the Ark of the Tabernacle with a throne protected by two angels, one standing on each side of the throne to guard it with outspread wings.[19]

At a Catholic church in one of the mid-Atlantic states, angels surround the tabernacle.[20] Large golden angels kneel before it on the left and right sides, while smaller silver angels stand on either side of the tabernacle door, hands folded in prayer. The smaller angels gaze at the door's predominant feature: a single cross resting on top of a circle formed by sheaves of wheat. A closer look reveals nails or thorns placed on diagonals to form an X within the circle. Tiny circles of vines separate the thorns and the arms of the cross within the larger circle. Behind the cross, bas-relief vines and grapes provide a highly textured surface. The prayer of the angels, "Sanctus, Sanctus, Sanctus" ("Holy, Holy, Holy"), that we join in at every Mass spans the top of the tabernacle, above the door and the silver angels. Those angels stand on water, spiritual beings held up by the Holy Spirit. In addition, another symbol of the Holy Spirit, a dove, descends upon the top of the tabernacle.

---

[18] Rozell, Lynda. "Angels in Chicago," *Tin Can Pilgrim blog* (Oct. 9, 2019), https://tincanpilgrim.com/2019/10/09/angels-in-chicago (photos and discussion of Saint Mary of the Angels Catholic Church in Chicago IL).

[19] Exod 25:18-22.

[20] The pastor gave permission for me to use my photograph of the tabernacle in this book but prefers anonymity for the name and location of the church.

Photograph 51—Catholic Church, Mid-Atlantic area of the U.S. Used with permission.

Another fine example, this time from a much smaller church, is found at Christ Our Redeemer Catholic Church in Niceville, Florida. Just as Catholics do when entering a church or pew, angels genuflect by kneeling on one knee before the central cross on the tabernacle. Natural light illuminates this golden cylindrical dwelling place of Jesus through the large windows that surround it in a side chapel. The beauty of God in the sky, trees, and foliage visible through the windows highlights His humility to be here with us so tangibly. From a flaming sun behind the cross, golden rays stream out to the edges of the tabernacle door. Borders of grapevines climb the tabernacle to a crown of fleurs-de-lis, symbol of the Trinity. The tabernacle's circular fluted top resembles a bell with the Holy Spirit descending upon it in the form of a dove.

Photograph 52—Christ Our Redeemer Catholic Church, Niceville, FL. Used with permission.

Prayer/Devotion

Reflect on how your own personal angel protects you. Recall the simplest childhood prayer, as a child of God:

Angel of God, my guardian dear,
to whom God's love commits me here.
Ever this day be at my side
to light and guard,
to rule and guide. Amen.

Imagine your guardian angel adoring and worshipping Jesus in the tabernacle with you. You can ask your angel to accompany you at any moment during the day even in small challenges such as finding a parking spot. You can also share your joys with your guardian angel, asking your angel to help you stay in the presence of Christ as you climb a trail or dance at a party.

Even Jesus, in his humanity, has a guardian angel. As Jesus suffers in the garden of Gethsemane, an angel appears to comfort and minister to Him. There, Jesus prays in full knowledge and anticipation of His coming passion, asking the Father to take this cup from Him yet fully accepting the Father's will. Although Jesus's disciples all fall asleep, His angel stays with Him as His sweat becomes like blood.[21]

We too can pray that Jesus's angel from the garden accompanies us when we watch over a loved one who is suffering. Use your own words or consider the traditional Prayer to the Angel of Gethsemane:

O Angel of Gethsemane, chosen by the Father to bring strength and consolation to Jesus during His agony, I ask you to be with me now as I keep watch over my loved one who is

---

[21] Luke 22:42-44.

sick and suffering. Help me to offer my best care, love and protection to this child of God. May my words and my touch be filled with gentleness, my presence bring comfort, and my prayers bring rest and healing sleep. Do what I cannot do, O loving Angel, to bring healing and strength to soul and body, according to the Father's will. Amen. [22]

---

[22] *See* Armstrong, Patti Maguire. "Did Jesus Have A Guardian Angel?" *National Catholic Register* blog (Oct 2, 2022), https://www.ncregister.com/blog/did-jesus-have-a-guardian-angel?amp.

CHAPTER EIGHT

The Church

Tabernacles occasionally image the Church, sometimes metaphorically and sometimes through architectural elements. Thus, some tabernacles essentially model the larger church building which houses them. Others show the apostles, usually with Jesus, as in scenes of the Last Supper, the Transfiguration, and other key moments in Jesus's ministry on Earth. Specifically, tabernacles often honor the four evangelists – Saints Matthew, Mark, Luke and John – among the apostles.

The Four Evangelists

Badges or symbols of the four evangelists and authors of the Gospels — Saint Matthew the Angel, Saint Mark the Lion, Saint Luke the Ox, and Saint John the Eagle — regularly are found on tabernacles as a motif representing the Church. In the Old Testament the prophet Ezekiel describes a vision of four-sided creatures: "their form was human, but each had four faces and four wings ... Each of the four had the face of a man, but on the right side was the face of a lion, and on the left side the face of an ox and finally each had the face of an eagle."[1] One of the early Church fathers, Saint Jerome, attributes each of these four faces to symbolize the evangelists: "The Gospel of Matthew begins with the Incarnation, so his symbol is a

---

[1] Ezek 1:5-6, 10.

man (or an angel). Mark begins his Gospel with John the Baptist whose "voice crying out in the wilderness" was as solitary and powerful as a lion's roar. Luke stressed the theme of sacrifice, so the figure of the ox was associated with him. And John's Gospel, according to Saint Jerome, achieved spiritual heights and therefore soared like an eagle."[2]

Likewise, the symbols of the evangelists also represent the four creatures that Revelation describes as surrounding God's throne. There "stood four living creatures covered with eyes front and back. The first creature resembled a lion; the second, an ox; the third had the face of a man; while the fourth looked like an eagle in flight. Each of the four living creatures had six wings and eyes all over, inside and out. Day and night, without pause, they sing: "Holy, holy, holy, is the Lord God Almighty, He who was, and who is, and who is to come!"[3] The parallels to Ezekiel's vision are striking.

Another one of the early Church Fathers, Saint Irenaeus, explains that Matthew's symbol is a divine man because his Gospel highlights Jesus's humanity and his entry into the world.[4] Further, Saint Irenaeus notes that Saint Mark begins his gospel with reference to Isaiah's prophecy of a voice in the desert crying which evokes a lion's roar – the voice of a creature symbolizing royalty.[5] Oxen were

---

[2] Sullivan, Charles T. "Four evangelists' symbols came from themes in their Gospels" *Arkansas Catholic* (May 5, 2007), https://www.dolr.org/article/four-evangelists%E2%80%99-symbols-came-themes-their-gospels.

[3] Rev 4:6-8.

[4] Saunders, Fr. William. "What Are the Symbols of the Four Evangelists?" *Catholic Exchange* (Aug. 19, 2020), https://catholicexchange.com/what-are-the-symbols-of-the-four-evangelists.

[5] *Id.*

Chapter Eight: The Church 131

used in temple sacrifice, such as Zechariah's sacrifice at the outset of the Gospel of Luke before an angel foretells the birth of John the Baptist. The parable of the Prodigal Son in Luke's Gospel also deals with sacrifice of the fatted calf, signifying joy through the sacrifice and mercy of Christ. Thus, the ox is the symbol of priestly sacrifice. Finally, Saint Irenaeus observes that John's Gospel "begins with the 'lofty' prologue of the Word and 'rises' to pierce most deeply the mysteries of God, the relationship between the Father and the Son, and the incarnation."[6]

Photograph 53—Blessed Sacrament Chapel, Cathedral of the Holy Cross, Boston, MA. Used with permission.

---

[6] *Id.*, citing Saint Irenaeus.

Symbols of the four evangelists decorate the tabernacle in the Blessed Sacrament Chapel at the Cathedral of the Holy Cross in Boston, Massachusetts. They surround the image of Christ the King seated on His throne. The kingship of Christ receives further emphasis in the peaked crown-like construction of the tabernacle, complete with jewels and a center medallion of the triumphant Lamb of God.

Photograph 54—St. Mary of the Immaculate Conception Catholic Church, Fredericksburg, VA. Used with permission.

Chapter Eight: The Church 133

At Saint Mary of the Immaculate Conception in Fredericksburg, Virginia, a beautiful gold tabernacle with silver and blue inlay provides an excellent example of the four evangelists' symbols. The door of the tabernacle richly embossed with patterns of grape leaves and vines balances the four symbols in circles around the arms of a central cross. Each figure has a halo and wings.

Photograph 55—Blessed Sacrament Chapel, Cathedral of St. Matthew the Apostle, Washington, DC. Used with permission.

Not far away, in Washington, D.C., a square gold, red, and white tabernacle with a domed roof rests on a white marble table. On its door four red squares depict in bas-relief gold the symbols of each of the four evangelists. This brilliantly decorated tabernacle in the Blessed Sacrament Chapel of the Cathedral of Saint Matthew the Apostle is in front of a wall covered by a fine red, gold, and blue mosaic of two disciples gazing joyfully at Jesus in the tabernacle. The words "They recognized him in the breaking of the bread" appear in the glittering mosaic. These words are from the testimony of two disciples who leave Jerusalem after Jesus's crucifixion, weary and discouraged.[7] They encounter our Risen Lord on the road to Emmaus, and, once they recognize Him, rush back to spread the news to the other disciples. The tabernacle bearing the images of the evangelists fits within the broader context of the rekindled faith and zeal of the disciples whom Jesus transforms into evangelists. Together, they remind us of Jesus's True Presence in the tabernacle hidden under the guise of bread, recognized only through the eyes of faith, inspiring us to bring Him to the world.

Prayer/Devotion

As with other motifs, church images on tabernacles can inspire our conversation with God. Let tabernacles depicting symbols of the four evangelists inspire you to select a passage from each Gospel for meditation. Ask Jesus to transform you, as He did the disciples on

---

[7] Luke 24:13-35.

Chapter Eight: The Church 135

the road to Emmaus, by opening the Scriptures to you and finding Him in the breaking of the bread.

Photograph 56—Blessed Sacrament Chapel, Cathedral of St. Matthew the Apostle, Washington, DC. Used with permission.

Pray for opportunities to witness to God's love and the Good News of salvation won for us by Jesus. The apostle Paul often asked others to pray for him.[8] So pray for one another as a community seeking to bring others to relationship with God. The First Letter of Peter urges Christians to "sanctify Christ's word in your hearts. Always be ready to give an explanation to anyone who asks you for a reason for your hope, but do so with gentleness and reverence."[9]

This advice remains true today. We can prepare ourselves to be ready with explanations, with reasons for our hope in Christ. Spiritual reading, including the Bible, helps us be familiar with our faith. The Catechism of the Catholic Church is a wonderful resource as is the podcast of the same name narrated by Father Mike Schmitz and produced by Ascension Press. Ultimately, however, it is the Holy Spirit working through our actions and words that converts hearts to share in our joy.

Cathedrals and Churches

Some tabernacles resemble small churches or depict cathedrals or the Heavenly City from Revelation. Many features of tabernacles borrow from features of church architecture, such as rounded domes or ceilings supported by pillars.[10] A few tabernacles even mimic a particular church or cathedral. For me, this design emphasizes the Real Presence of the Lord in the tabernacle. Just as we are

---

[8] *See, e.g.*, Col 4:2-4 ("pray for us, too, that God may open a door to us for the word, to speak of the mystery of Christ").

[9] 1 Pet 3:15-16.

[10] *See, e.g.*, discussion of tabernacle at Saint Francis of Assisi in La Quinta, California, in Chapter Six.

present within the church building, He is present sacramentally within the replica of the building.

Photograph 57—Ave Maria Catholic Church, Ave Maria, FL. Used with permission.

    For example, Ave Maria Catholic Church in southwest Florida boasts a unique design in the shape of a bishop's mitre, a tall, tapered hat. The tabernacle repeats this theme, adding the color blue to honor Mary.

    Similarly, in West Virginia, the tabernacle of Saint James the Greater Catholic Church in Charles Town looks just like the exterior of the church itself, except that the tabernacle door has a golden cross. As we enter through the doors of the church, Christ in the consecrated host enters into the door of the tabernacle.

*Photograph 58—St. James the Greater, Charles Town, WV.
Used with permission.*

Other church-like tabernacles evoke buildings in general, like the early tower style tabernacles. For example, the tabernacle in the chapel of the Cathedral of the Immaculate Conception in Portland,

Chapter Eight: The Church 139

Maine, has elaborate neo-Gothic carved columns below an open roof.

Photograph 59—Cathedral of the Immaculate Conception Chapel, Portland, ME. Used with permission.

Likewise, at Saint Mary's Catholic Church in Jackson, Tennessee, pictured on the following page, a miniature white and gray marble domed building encases a peaked wooden tabernacle. The arched tabernacle door bears a golden sculpted image of the host and chalice against a field of blue. The juxtaposition of these elements gives the illusion of a tabernacle within a simple wooden church within an imposing marble basilica. Jesus is with us, in the humblest of settings as well as the grandest.

Prayer/Devotion

*Photograph 60—St. Mary Catholic Church, Jackson, TN.
Used with permission.*

As with other tabernacle themes, church imagery can inspire our conversation with God as we visit Jesus in His Real Presence. It reminds us to pray for the Church, for vocations to the priesthood and

Chapter Eight: The Church 141

religious life, for the Holy Spirit to fill the laity with zeal to share the Good News and to live out their faith in daily life. We can also pray for our particular parish and our priests, for the pope and bishops, and for all those who serve the Church as deacons, ministers, lectors, sacristans, cantors, musicians, catechists, teachers, and volunteers in its charitable and spiritual activities.

Here are a few prayers that may lead you deeper into prayer for the Church. Saint Therese's prayer for priests is a favorite of mine. Also, the prayer to Saint Joseph asking for intercession for the whole Church reminds us that we are a community and everyone in the Church has a role to play.

Saint Therese or the "Little Flower" is a Doctor of the Church, renowned for her simple and direct spirituality. She determined to pray for priests when she took her final vows as a Carmelite nun and called herself "an apostle of the apostles."[11] Saint Therese is the patron saint of priests and missionaries. Although she longed to be a missionary herself, she did not reach that goal in her earthly life. Instead, she spiritually adopted priests and devoted herself to supporting missionaries with prayer.[12] You can join her in this prayer often attributed to her:[13]

---

[11] Seitz, Rev. Wolfgang. "St. Therese and the Priesthood" Saint Therese Church (Alhambra CA) website, http://www.stthereschurchalhambra.org/?DivisionID=10357&DepartmentID=25315.

[12] *Id.*

[13] *See* USCCB, *The Saint Therese Vocation Society Brochure* (Diocese of Arlington Office of Vocations), https://www.usccb.org/beliefs-and-teachings/vocations/vocation-directors/upload/st-terese-vocation-society-adult-english.pdf.

O Jesus, I pray for your faithful and fervent priests;
>   for your unfaithful and tepid priests;
>   for your priests laboring at home or abroad in distant mission fields;
>   for your tempted priests;
>   for your lonely and desolate priests;
>   for your young priests;
>   for your dying priests;
>   for the souls of your priests in Purgatory.

But above all, I recommend to you the priests dearest to me:
>   the priest who baptized me;
>   the priests who've absolved me from my sins;
>   the priests at whose Masses I've assisted and who've given me Your Body and Blood in Holy Communion;
>   the priests who've taught and instructed me;
>   all the priests to whom I am indebted in any other way, especially ____ (provide names)

O Jesus, keep them all close to your heart,
>   and bless them abundantly in time and in eternity. Amen.

Some view Saint Joseph as the protector of the keys to the tabernacle because he protects Jesus in the tabernacle just as he protects the Church and protected his wife Mary and the infant Jesus.[14] As

---

[14] Saint Josemaria, the founder of Opus Dei, prayed for Saint Joseph's intercession that the first oratory of Opus Dei would be permitted to reserve the Blessed Sacrament in its tabernacle. In gratitude, Saint Josemaria

Chapter Eight: The Church 143

the patron saint of homes, it only makes sense that Saint Joseph would watch over the dwelling of the Real Presence of Jesus in every tabernacle. The following prayer to Saint Joseph asks him to intercede for the pope, the bishops, priests, and the whole Church:[15]

> O Glorious Saint Joseph,
> you were chosen by God
> to be the foster father of Jesus,
> the most pure spouse of Mary, ever Virgin,
> and the head of the Holy Family.
> You have been chosen by Christ's Vicar
> as the heavenly Patron and Protector
> of the Church founded by Christ.
>
> Protect the Sovereign Pontiff
> and all bishops and priests united with him.
> Be the protector of all who labour for souls
> amid the trials and tribulations of this life;
> and grant that all peoples of the world
> may be docile to the Church
> without which there is no salvation.

---

asked that centers of Opus Dei attach a small medal of Saint Joseph to each tabernacle key with the inscription *Ite ad Joseph* (Go to Joseph). Saint Josemaria wanted this to be a reminder that just as Joseph in the Old Testament was the key to feeding the people of Israel in famine, so Saint Joseph "provided us with the most precious nourishment of all: the Holy Eucharist." Opus Dei, *Meditations: First Sunday of Saint Joseph* (Jan. 29, 2023), https://opusdei.org/en/article/first-sunday-of-saint-joseph/.

[15] See "Prayer to Saint Joseph for the Whole Church," *Catholic.org*, https://www.catholic.org/prayers/prayer.php?p=587.

Dear Saint Joseph,
accept the offering I make to you.
Be my father, protector,
and guide in the way of salvation.
Obtain for me purity of heart
and a love for the spiritual life.
After your example,
let all my actions be directed
to the greater glory of God,
in union with the Divine Heart of Jesus,
the Immaculate Heart of Mary,
and your own paternal heart.

Finally, pray for me that I may share
in the peace and joy of your holy death.

Amen.

Photograph 61—Tabernacle Key, Riverside Study Center Oratory, New York City, NY. Photograph by Brian Finnerty. Used with permission.

CHAPTER NINE

Mission

The Church is not stagnant. We are a missionary Church that the Spirit sets aflame with Christ's love to share it with others. Mission as a theme in tabernacles expresses itself through one of the oldest Christian symbols, the fish, as well as in more modern depictions such as the globe. Finally, mission as a tabernacle theme finds its highest expression in the living tabernacles we become after receiving Christ in the Eucharist. Like Mary, we bear Christ to others.

Fish

In His earliest call to mission, Jesus invites Simon (Peter), Andrew, James, and John to follow Him and promises they will become fishers of men.[1] After directing a dubious Peter to "put out into deep water and lower your nets for a catch," Jesus fills the nets with so many fish that the boat nearly capsizes.[2] When we follow Jesus, and empty our hands to accept His outstretched ones, He fills them abundantly just like He filled the nets with fish. After the Resurrection, Jesus meets the disciples at the end of a fruitless night of fishing on their own. He instructs them to cast their nets on the other side of their boat. Again, when they follow His direction, the nets fill to

---

[1] Luke 5:10-11.
[2] Luke 5:4-7.

bursting, and Peter recognizes, "It is the Lord."[3] Fish thus symbolize the Church's mission, led by Jesus as Head, to bring the good news of salvation to all.

Photographs 62 and 63—Sacred Heart Catholic Church, Bloomfield, NJ. Images from website used with permission.

Several images of fish and fishing may be found on tabernacles representing the evangelism of the Church, the mission of setting out into the deep to bring others to Christ. For instance, the Greek word fish or *ichthus* refers to Jesus Christ. Saint Augustine explains that, "If you join the initial letters of these five Greek words Iesous Christos Theou Uios Soter – which mean Jesus Christ, Son of God, Saviour – they will form the word ichthus, that is 'fish,' the word by which Christ is mystically understood because He was able to live, that is, to exist without sin in the abyss of this mortality as in the

---

[3] *See* John 21:4-12.

Chapter Nine: Mission 147

depth of waters." The word "fish" also, of course, is the command He gave to Peter, first with reference to actual fish, then figuratively with regard to men.

At Sacred Heart Catholic Church in Bloomfield, New Jersey, the ichthus appears as one of several Christian symbols on the tabernacle's door. While this book includes some of them, the church's website explains all the symbols on its tabernacle, including the unicorn, peacock, and phoenix.[4]

Photograph 64—Blessed Trinity Catholic Church, Frankenmuth, MI. Used with permission.

---

[4] Sacred Heart Catholic Church, *The Tabernacle*, https://www.shc-bloomfield.org/the-tabernacle.

By contrast to the multiplicity of symbols on the tabernacle at Sacred Heart, the tabernacle at Blessed Trinity Catholic Church in Frankenmuth, Michigan, focuses on fish. An entire school of fish seems to jump and swirl on a carved wooden tabernacle in the Blessed Sacrament chapel. The peaked light resting above the fish resembles the top of a lighthouse, reminding us that we, like Jesus, are to be a light to the world. The triangular sides of the light also suggest the Trinity. Together, these design elements embody the call to go out into the deep as fishers of men and invite all to relationship with the Holy Trinity.

Use of the fish symbol in churches is widespread, but appears more often on other liturgical furnishings than on tabernacles. This altar rail at Saint Anthony's Catholic Church in North Beach, Maryland, is a good example. The simplicity of the fish outline recalls how early Christians used a fish formed by two arcs to identify one another as followers of Christ during times of persecution.[5]

Both Catholics and Protestants use the fish symbol, making it a sign of unity as well as mission in our post-Christian world. For example, *The Chosen*, a popular drama about Jesus and His apostles, uses fish swimming against the current in its logo and introduction. The series relates the stories of the Gospels by focusing on the apostles and how Jesus transforms them into missionaries for the Kingdom. We all share in that mission.

---

[5] Zahorik, Lyn. "Fish symbol has deep roots," *The Compass* (Diocese of Green Bay Wisconsin: Feb. 7, 2013), https://www.thecompassnews.org/2013/02/fish-symbol-has-deep-roots.

Chapter Nine: Mission

Photograph 65—St. Anthony's Catholic Church, North Beach, MD. Used with permission.

Unity

When we receive Jesus in the Eucharist, we not only experience communion with Him but with all others receiving Communion. Our "Amen" proclaimed in response to the priest's declaration of "The Body of Christ" says we agree, we are unified with the Catholic Church, and we believe this is the Body of Christ. As the eucharistic prayer in the Catholic liturgy states, "Grant that we, who are nourished by his body and blood, may be filled with his Holy Spirit, and become one body, one spirit in Christ."[6]

Thus, the sacramental Body and Blood of Christ does more than strengthen us individually; it strengthens the Body of Christ as a whole. "The Eucharist is the sacrament and the source of the

---

[6] Eucharistic Prayer III, *The Roman Missal* (3rd ed.). New Jersey: Catholic Book Publishing. 2011.

Church's unity,"[7] said Saint John Paul II. Saint Paul expresses this as follows: "Because there is one bread, we who are many are one body, for we all partake of the one bread."[8] He urges the Ephesians to exercise humility, gentleness, and patience, "bearing with one another through love, striving to preserve the unity of the spirit through the bond of peace: one body and one Spirit, as you were also called to the one hope of your call; one Lord, one faith, one baptism; one God and Father of all, who is over all and through all and in all."[9]

Elaborating on how the Eucharist helps us live in unity and charity, the Archbishop of Baltimore, William E. Lori, explains: "Since the Eucharist makes us one in Christ, it strengthens our love and respect for one another. Having been nourished by the Lord Himself, we should, with an active love, strive to eliminate all prejudices and obstacles to brotherly cooperation with others."[10] Although imperfect and often troubled by dissent and disunity, the Church in its diversity is modeled after the Trinity in terms of representing unity of the three persons in one God. The Church brings the Eucharist to us as "a sacrament of unity and charity" that binds us together in love. "In the power of the Holy Spirit, the crucified and risen Lord draws us to himself and unites us with his heavenly Father and with

---

[7] Pope Saint John Paul II, General Audience 11.8.2000, https://www.vatican.va/content/john-paul-ii/en/audiences/2000/documents/hf_jp-ii_aud_20001108.html.

[8] 1 Cor 10:17.

[9] Eph 4:1-6.

[10] Lori, Archbishop William E. "Eucharist: Sacrament of Unity," *Catholic Review* (June 11, 2021), https://catholicreview.org/eucharist-sacrament-of-unity.

Chapter Nine: Mission

one another. As ancient Christian writers often said, 'The Eucharist makes the Church.' It continuously brings into being the communion of love and life that is the Church."[11]

The unity manifested by the Eucharist extends not only to communion with one another within the Catholic Church, but through the grace of the Holy Spirit, we are to seek to "strengthen the bonds of communion between all Christians,"[12] as Saint John Paul II wrote. We are to focus on what unites us, not what divides.[13]

Thus, unity begins with our own individual union with Christ, God the Father, and the Holy Spirit, then extends to unity with others in the Catholic Church, then to unity with all others who believe in Jesus. Finally, unity is integral to mission: Jesus asks us to go out to the whole world and invite them to become one with Him.

As we visit tabernacles, we can reflect upon the prayer of Jesus for his disciples before His Ascension: "I pray not only for them, but also for those who will believe in me through their word, so that they may all be one, as you, Father, are in me and I in you, that they also may be in us, that the world may believe that you sent me. And I have given them the glory you gave me, so that they may be one, as we are one, I in them and you in me, that they may be brought to perfection as one, that the world may know that you sent me, and that you loved them even as you loved me."[14]

---

[11] *Id.*

[12] Pope Saint John Paul II, *Ut Unum Sint* (May 25, 1995) at 101, https://www.vatican.va/content/john-paul-ii/en/encyclicals/documents/hf_jp-ii_enc_25051995_ut-unum-sint.html.

[13] *Id.* at 22 (encouraging common prayer).

[14] John 17:20-23.

As I traveled, I found several tabernacles shaped like globes. The image of the globe expresses the unity of the body of Christ. Just as we are one Catholic Church, with many different cultures and peoples, the globe contains all the countries and continents of the Earth. The variety of globe tabernacles seems to capture this sense of being one despite our differences.

Photograph 66—St. Thomas Catholic Church, Staten Island, NY. Used with permission.

Chapter Nine: Mission 153

Several years ago, I found a beautiful example of a globe tabernacle within a side chapel at Saint Thomas Catholic Church in Staten Island, New York.[15] The outer tabernacle shaped like a globe contains a smaller tabernacle inside of it bearing images of loaves and fishes, a theme discussed in Chapter Four.[16] On the globe, longitude and latitude lines mark a grid on which the continents of the Earth rest, just as we rest in God's hands.

Photographs 67 and 68—St. Oscar Romero Parish, Canton, MA. Used with permission.

Another distinctive globe-shaped tabernacle stands within a small adoration chapel at Saint Oscar Romero Parish in Canton, Massachusetts. A smooth gold surface bears a silver Chi Rho and the alpha and omega symbols. Placement of this tabernacle in an alcove

---

[15] This tabernacle no longer is in use at Saint Thomas, but is in a sacred art repository owned by the Archdiocese of New York.

[16] *See* Chapter Four (discussion of loaves and fishes).

beneath a statue of Mary reminds us that Our Mother is watching over the world.

Much farther south, in Mount Dora, Florida, at Saint Patrick Catholic Church, a gold and silver globe tabernacle shows the continents, but the main feature is the cross from which rays of light spread over the world. This striking tabernacle embodies the idea of Christ unifying the world with his love and light.

Like the light streaming over the earth from the cross, the Eucharist embraces us in grace, creating unity with Christ and one another. "Those who receive the Eucharist are united more closely to Christ. Through it, Christ unites them to all the faithful in one body – the Church." [17]

Photograph 69—St. Patrick Catholic Church, Mount Dora, FL. Used with permission.

---

[17] CCC 1396.

How fitting that Christ in His Real Presence, in this sacrament of unity, occasionally dwells inside a globe.

Prayer/Devotion

Any of the Scripture passages cited above can be read slowly and provide a rich source of reflection. Pray for unity and peace in your own home, in your family, with your neighbors, within our country, and across the entire world.

I particularly like the prayer for unity from the Diocese of San Angelo, Texas. This prayer by an anonymous author draws inspiration from the Eucharistic Prayer for Reconciliation:

> Eternal Father, source of love,
> by your Holy Spirit you move human hearts
> so that enemies may speak to each other again,
> adversaries join hands,
> hatred is overcome by love,
> revenge gives way to forgiveness,
> and discord is changed to mutual respect.
> Grant us, through the action of the Spirit,
> the grace to contribute,
> together with all people of good will,
> to the fulfillment of your Son's will:
> "That they may all be one!"
> With faith, we ask you for the divine gift of unity.
> Give us enough love and courage
> to seek to overcome disunity,
> whether it is friction in our families, tensions in our neighborhood,

disagreements at work, in our parish, or among different religious groups.
Help us to enter into honest and respectful dialogue.
Keep us from being indifferent.
Soften our hearts. Open our ears.
Help us to listen with close attention to the other person,
sharing in the pain caused by their wounds.
Help us to build bridges rather than walls.
Make us instruments of your peace.
We humbly pray to you:
allow us, your children,
to live in solidarity with all people
and so to honor you, who are the Father of us all.
We ask these things through Jesus Christ,
in the unity of the Most Holy Trinity.
Amen.[18]

Living Tabernacles: Bearing Christ to the World

Many tabernacles honor Mary, the Mother of God, through images of the Annunciation, stars, or use of the color blue. Mary's "yes" to God's plan of salvation through Jesus Christ's incarnation allowed Jesus through the Holy Spirit to be conceived in her womb. She thus became the first eucharistic tabernacle, carrying Jesus in her womb.[19]

---

[18] *Prayer for Unity: Anonymous Meditation Based on Eucharistic Prayer for Reconciliation II*, Diocese of San Angelo website, https://sanangelodiocese.org/prayer-for-unity. Used with permission.

[19] *See* discussion in Chapter Two.

Chapter Nine: Mission

The Scriptural parallels between Mary as the new Ark and the old Ark of the Covenant are striking. In the Old Testament, the Ark carries the Word of God in the tablets bearing the Ten Commandments; in the New, Mary carries the Word of God incarnate. Upon learning that her aged cousin Elizabeth is pregnant, Mary goes in haste to the hill country to help her. As Mary approaches, the unborn baby, John the Baptist, leaps in Elizabeth's womb,[20] just as David leaps and dances before the ark when it comes to Jerusalem.[21] Elizabeth exclaims, "Who am I that the mother of my Lord should come to me?"[22] echoing David's cry, "How can the Ark of the Lord come to me?"[23]

Note that Elizabeth proclaims joy while David expresses fear of God's wrath, illustrating how God throughout time teaches His people how to be in relationship with Him. It took many generations of preparation for the Messiah to come as a vulnerable infant, to save us and establish a kingdom beyond the expectations of His people.[24]

---

[20] Luke 1:44.
[21] 2 Sam 6:3-5.
[22] Luke 1:43.
[23] 2 Sam 6:9.
[24] There are many other foreshadowings of the New Testament in the Old Testament related to Mary. For example, David left the ark with a foreigner outside Jerusalem in the hill country for 3 months (2 Samuel 6:10-11); Mary spent 3 months with Elizabeth in the hill country (Luke 1:56). *See* Armstrong, Dave. "Amazing Parallels Between Mary and the Ark of the Covenant," *National Catholic Register* (Feb. 13, 2018), https://www.ncregister.com/blog/amazing-parallels-between-mary-and-the-ark-of-the-covenant?amp. For more comprehensive examination of how the Old Testament foreshadows the New and the New Testament fulfills the Old, see Cavins, Jeff, *et al. A Catholic Guide to the Old Testament,*

We go to Jesus through Mary. She can help us adore Him and bear Him to the world as living tabernacles. You can find strength and grace at tabernacles. Imitating Mary, you can find inspiration to follow Her Son at Marian-themed tabernacles.

Photograph 70—St. Mary of the Immaculate Conception, Fredericksburg, VA. Used with permission.

For example, in Fredericksburg, Virginia, at Saint Mary of the Immaculate Conception Catholic Church, the ornate tabernacle in-

---

(Ascension Press 2023) and Hahn, Scott, *The Fourth Cup: Unveiling the Mystery of the Last Supper and the Cross* (Image 2018).

Chapter Nine: Mission   159

corporates blue medallions and fields of blue to honor Mary. Likewise, Ave Maria Catholic Church's tabernacle, pictured earlier in Chapter Eight, expresses devotion to Mary through use of the color blue.

Photograph 71—St. Stanislaus Kostka Catholic Church, Chicago, IL. Image from parish website. Used with permission.

In Chicago, Saint Stanislaus Kostka Catholic Church commissioned a beautiful piece of art that honors Mary as the dwelling place of Christ. It is a monstrance on top of a tabernacle. The tabernacle evokes the Ark of the Covenant, following in miniature the description God provides to Moses, complete with angels gazing at the tabernacle in worship. The tabernacle door bears images of what the old ark contained: the tablets of the Ten Commandments, a bowl of manna, and Aaron's staff. Manna, the bread that fell like dewfall in the desert to nourish the Israelites, foreshadows the Eucharist. A statue of Mary, the new ark, on top of the tabernacle displays Jesus in the Blessed Sacrament for adoration.

*Photograph 72—Our Lady of Good Counsel, Plymouth, MI.
Used with permission.*

*Photograph 73—Our Lady of Good Counsel, Plymouth, MI.
Used with permission.*

Chapter Nine: Mission

Similarly, the tabernacle of Our Lady of Good Counsel Catholic Church in Plymouth, Michigan, resembles the ark of the covenant. It makes literal the parallels we find in Scripture by including the image of Mary's Annunciation on the doors of the tabernacle. To inspire further delight in the mystery of the Eucharist, the wall to the left of the tabernacle displays the Hebrew words Isaac asks his father Jacob on the way to sacrifice, "Where is the Lamb?"[25] To the right of the tabernacle we see the Greek words answering this question — "Behold the Lamb of God"[26] — that John the Baptist uses to identify Jesus as the Messiah.

Through grace, we can be like Mary and bring Christ to the world, through our actions and words, through acts of charity both corporal and spiritual. Feeding the hungry is more than bringing them ordinary food. We can bring the message that they are loved as sons and daughters of God and invite them to pray and to discover and strengthen their relationship with Him. Mary helps us bring others to Her Son, sometimes by providing a friendlier focus to someone traumatized by their own father who may struggle to see anyone, including God, as a good father.

Marian tabernacles remind us to go to Mary and ask for her help and her prayers for our intentions. She brings our problems to her Son, just as she did at Cana when the wedding hosts ran short of wine. Jesus did not deny her request even though it may not have been His original plan to start his public ministry at that point.[27]

---

[25] Gen 22:7.

[26] John 1:29.

[27] John 2:1-11, "When the wine ran short, the mother of Jesus said to him, 'They have no wine.' [And] Jesus said to her, 'Woman, how does your

Mary's message to us, as to the servants at the wedding, is to "do whatever He tells you." This is a fitting point for contemplating mission as a tabernacle theme and our own purpose in life.

Prayer/Devotion:

You may wish to reflect on scenes from the Rosary, specifically the mysteries of the Annunciation and the Visitation.[28]

Pray the traditional prayer asking for Mary's intercession, the *Memorare*:

> Remember, O most gracious Virgin Mary, that never was it known that anyone who fled to thy protection, implored thy help, or sought thine intercession, was left unaided.
> Inspired by this confidence I fly unto thee, O Virgin of virgins, my Mother.
> To thee do I come, before thee I stand, sinful and sorrowful.
> O Mother of the Word Incarnate, despise not my petitions, but in thy mercy hear and answer me.
> Amen.[29]

---

concern affect me? My hour has not yet come.' His mother said to the servers, 'Do whatever he tells you.'"

[28] *See* Chapter Six for more information about the Rosary and how to meditate on its mysteries.

[29] USCCB, Basic Prayers: Memorare, https://www.usccb.org/prayers/memorare.

Chapter Nine: Mission

Use your own words to talk with your Mother Mary from your heart. Here's an example from my prayer that you may borrow or that may lead you to your own conversation with her:

Mary, my mother given to me by Jesus on the cross, pray for me that I may have the grace to bear Jesus to the world as you did. May I reflect Him, point to Him, in all I do and say. Mary, the first living tabernacle, pray for all who receive your Son in the Blessed Sacrament, that they may do so worthily and with great benefit to their souls. May we as living tabernacles go forth to share Christ with others.

PART THREE

CONCLUSION

CHAPTER TEN

Where Our Hearts Find Rest

Despite diverse themes and different locations, all tabernacles essentially are the same. Jesus dwells there and He is the same today and always. For me, it is love of Jesus in the Eucharist that leads me to look for the tabernacle in every church I visit. It isn't the box itself; it is who lives there. You'll find many resources on the Eucharistic Revival website that can prompt your prayer and help you appreciate the Real Presence of Christ in the Eucharist.[1] Yet no matter how much you read or listen to explanations, it is not enough. Time in front of the tabernacle is what allows information to transform itself into love, for seeds to bloom into relationship. All relationships require time spent together.

Although the Father, the Son, and the Holy Spirit are outside of time, Jesus in His humanity entered into time. In this sense, each and every tabernacle where Jesus dwells is a time machine. He draws us in, He seeks us first, that we may respond by seeking Him.

We find Him everywhere, in our hearts, in others, in nature, in art, in the small tasks of each day. He is with us in grand cathedrals, in dances, processions, parties, and songs rejoicing in His beauty, power, mercy, and glory. We see Him in quiet cemeteries, in fountains of water, in labyrinths, in all that wakes us up and opens our eyes and hearts so we can perceive His Presence with us in every moment.

---

[1] *See* https://www.eucharisticrevival.org/.

The tabernacle focuses our longing to be with Him. In the guise of bread, He is sacramentally, physically incarnate, literally there. Spending time with Him at the tabernacle foreshadows when we will see Him face to face in person, in eternity.

Moreover, His Real Presence in the tabernacles we visit inspires us to be like Him and Mary, to be the Church, to go out on mission. "The tabernacle in church is immovable, but the human tabernacle is mobile. When a person is dismissed at the end of Mass and leaves the church, the communicant is to be like the Blessed Virgin Mary, the Christ-bearer, the one who brought Christ to the world. We are to bring Christ to those we meet. With Christ dwelling within us, the love of Christ should radiate outward from ourselves to others in our kindness, service and joy."[2]

Thus, we are called to be tabernacles to the world. That mission is nourished by receiving the Eucharist, by the sacrifice of Christ, and through our deep friendship with Him.

Think of your own experience with friendship. We all have dear friends we immediately pick up with after an absence as if we'd never been separated. We know each other on a deep level.

There's a hunger in us to be known because we are made for relationship. As Adam exclaimed in the Garden when meeting Eve: "This one, at last, is bone of my bones, and flesh of my flesh."[3] We find a similar recognition in friendship when we just click with

---

[2] Van Sloun, Rev. Michael. "Tabernacles Inside and Outside of Church," *The Catholic Spirit* (Nov. 21, 2019), reviewed August 29, 2023 at https://thecatholicspirit.com/faith/focus-on-faith/faith-fundamentals/tabernacles-inside-and-outside-of-church.

[3] Gen 2:23.

someone. Perhaps we like the same silly puns or a nerdy TV show or share a deep passion for chocolate cake. But on a deeper level, we see each other with all our qualities and flaws. We have history, we spend time together, we nourish that friendship by visiting, calling, writing, even texting.

Even when parted by death or distance, we "see" our friend through reminders that appear unexpectedly, like a bouquet of their favorite yellow flowers. We can speak with a departed or distant friend in our thoughts and sense their enduring love. A faithful friend is a sturdy shelter, as the psalmist writes.[4] Such a friend is a true treasure who can encourage and walk with us to holiness. We are made for relationship. Marriage, family relationship, and friendship are all forms of relationship that can lead us together to relationship in, with, and through God.

Divine intimacy grows in the same way friendship grows: by spending time together, by remembering our Divine Friend throughout the day, and by sharing our joys and sorrows. Unlike our human friends, however, Jesus has no flaws. Friendship with Him is perfect because He is perfect, even when we stumble. As Saint Josemaria reflects:

> Think of the human experience of two people who love each other, and yet are forced to part. They would like to stay together forever, but duty — in one form or another — forces them to separate. They are unable to fulfil their desire of remaining close to each other, so man's love — which, great as

---

[4] *See* Sir 6:14-17 (true friendship).

it may be, is limited — seeks a symbolic gesture. People who make their farewells exchange gifts or perhaps a photograph with a dedication so ardent that it seems almost enough to burn that piece of paper. They can do no more because a creature's power is not as great as its desire.

What we cannot do, our Lord is able to do. Jesus Christ, perfect God and perfect man, leaves us, not a symbol, but a reality. He himself stays with us. He will go to the Father, but he will also remain among men.[5]

Thus, our most beloved, best friend, and Lord Jesus stays with us in the tabernacle. He calls us to return to Him every day, to begin again when we fail or forget Him. With His infinite mercy, He invites us not only to visit Him, but through the Sacrament of Reconciliation to renew our relationship with Him and with one another.

We meet Jesus in others who love Him, in those who suffer, in innocent children, in the poor. We love Him in others and in ourselves. Each time you visit with Jesus Christ in His sacramental presence deepens and enriches that friendship. Jesus always "gets" us, unlike other friends who sometimes misinterpret or mistake what we do or say. We love Him, we seek to know Him more, to gaze into His eyes, to hold His hands, to rest in His arms. We can do so spiritually and await with joy the day when we shall be united fully in person. Meanwhile, He leaves us Himself to spend time with and

---

[5] *Christ is Passing By: Homilies by Saint Josemaria Escriva* (Scepter Pubs 1974), 83. Available online at https://escriva.org/en/es-cristo-que-pasa/83.

gives us the opportunity to receive Him in the most intimate relationship possible on Earth.

Our hunger to be known in relationship with others ultimately finds satisfaction in and with Jesus. But this is not a relationship that turns inward, that remains just between us as individuals and Jesus. He calls us to bring others into relationship with Him and with us. May your visits to His tabernacles ignite a flame of love within you to share Him with the world.

REFERENCES

3 Scriptures to Pray Every Evening, Scripture Lullabies (Nov 12, 2020), https://scripture-lullabies.com/3-scriptures-to-pray-every-evening.

Aleteia, "Why Are There Anchors in Christian Art?" *Aleteia*, https://aleteia.org/2017/06/10/why-are-there-anchors-in-christian-art.

Armenio, Peter V. *Highlights of the Catholic Faith*. 1st ed. Illinois: Midwest Theological Forum, 2023.

Armstrong, Dave. "Amazing Parallels Between Mary and the Ark of the Covenant," *National Catholic Register* (Feb. 13, 2018), https://www.ncregister.com/blog/amazing-parallels-between-mary-and-the-ark-of-the-covenant?amp

Armstrong, Patti Maguire. "Did Jesus Have A Guardian Angel?" *National Catholic Register* blog (Oct 2, 2022), https://www.ncregister.com/blog/did-jesus-have-a-guardian-angel?amp.

Barnes, Arthur. (1909). "Dove." In *The Catholic Encyclopedia*. New York: Robert Appleton Company. http://www.newadvent.org/cathen/ 05144b.htm

Bernock, Danielle. "The Celtic Cross – Its Origin and Meaning," Christianity.com, (July 5, 2019) https://www.christianity.com/church/what-is-the-celtic-cross-its-origin-and-meaning.html#google_vignette.

Bianchi, Hanael. "Bernini's baldacchino is actually a ciborium," *Catholic Review* (Dec. 2, 2020), https://catholicreview.org/berninis-baldacchino-is-actually-a-ciborium.

Burbidge, Most Rev. Michael F., Bishop of Arlington. *33 Spiritual Reflections for Daily Living* (Diocese of Arlington), https://www.arlingtondiocese.org/catechetical-resources/catechetical-messages-from-most-rev--michael-f--burbidge/.

Burbidge, Most Rev. Michael F., Bishop of Arlington. Pastoral Letter of Most Reverend Michael F. Burbidge, Bishop of Arlington. *In Tongues All Can Hear: Communicating the Hope of Christ in Times of Trial* (Sept. 15, 2020), https://www.arlingtondiocese.org/in-tongues-all-can-hear.

Candler, Very Rev. Sam. "Homily on the Fourth Sunday of Easter: The Shepherd is a Lamb," website of the Cathedral of Saint Philip, Atlanta, Georgia (April 30, 2023), https://www.cathedralatl.org/sermons/the-shepherd-is-a-lamb.

Castagnoli, Christopher. "A Prayer of Thanksgiving After Communion," *Our Catholic Prayers*, https://www.ourcatholicprayers.com/thanksgiving-after-communion.html.

Catholic Church. *Catechism of the Catholic Church: Revised in Accordance with the Official Latin Text Promulgated by Pope John Paul II*. United States Catholic Conference, 2000.

Catholic Encyclopedia, "Anchors symbolize hope," https://newadvent.org/cathen/01462a.htm.

Cavins, Jeff, et al. *A Catholic Guide to the Old Testament* (Ascension Press 2023)

Code of Canon Law, 1917.

Code of Canon Law, 1983.

Compass News. "One of the older 'secret' symbols of the faith," *Compass News* (Nov. 23, 2011).

References

D'Ambrosio, Marcellino. "Behold the Lamb of God: Reflection for the Second Sunday in Ordinary Time, Catholic Mom Holy Cross Family Ministries," (January 14, 2017), https://www.catholicmom.com/articles/2017/01/14/behold-lamb-god-reflection-second-sunday-ordinary-time.

Darcy, Peter. "What Does the IHS Symbol Really Mean?" *Catholic Stand* (Sept. 14, 2022), https://catholicstand.com/what-does-the-ihs-symbol-really-mean.

Diocese of Arlington, "Come and Rest Awhile, A Guide to Praying with Jesus in the Blessed Sacrament, compiled by Women Religious in the Diocese of Arlington" (2021), https://www.arlingtondiocese.org/communications/ado-ration-guide-final.pdf.

Diocese of Arlington, Holy Thursday 7 Churches Pilgrimage Adult Reflections, https://www.arlingtondiocese.org/uploadedfiles/cda/pages/youth_ministry/young_adult_ministry/7cp_booklet_eng_adult2023crop.pdf.

Diocese of San Angelo, Prayer for Unity: Anonymous Meditation Based on Eucharistic Prayer for Reconciliation II, Diocese of San Angelo website, https://sanangelodiocese.org/prayer-for-unity.

Dunn, Matthew. "The Prominence and Placement of Tabernacles Explained" (July 18, 2018), https://media.ascensionpress.com/2018/07/18/the-prominence-and-placement-of-tabernacles-explained/.

Escriva, Saint Josemaria. *The Way of the Cross*. (Scepter Publishers 1981).

Escriva, Saint Josemaria. *Christ is Passing By: Homilies by Saint Josemaria Escriva* (Scepter Pubs 1974), 83. Available online at https://escriva.org/en/es-cristo-que-pasa/83.

Eucharistic Prayer III, *The Roman Missal* (3rd ed.). New Jersey: Catholic Book Publishing. 2011.

Fitzgerald, Sally, Editor. *Letters of Flannery O'Connor: The Habit of Being*. (Farrar, Straus and Giroux, 1988) at 125.

Hahn, Scott. *The Fourth Cup: Unveiling the Mystery of the Last Supper and the Cross* (Image 2018).

Hassett, Maurice. "The Lamb (in Early Christian Symbolism)." *The Catholic Encyclopedia*. Vol. 8. New York: Robert Appleton Company, 1910. 18 Aug. 2023. http://www.newadvent.org/cathen/08755b.htm.

Hassett, Maurice. "The Anchor (as Symbol)." *The Catholic Encyclopedia*. Vol. 1. New York: Robert Appleton Company, 1907, http://www.newadvent.org/cathen/01462a.htm.

Hermes, Kathryn J. "God has come to seek me out" *National Eucharistic Revival Blog* (Dec. 20, 2022), https://www.eucharisticrevival.org/post/god-has-come-to-seek-me-out.

Hoffman, Rev. Francis. "Where Should the Tabernacle Be?" *Simply Catholic*, https://www.simplycatholic.com/where-should-the-tabernacle-be.

Hymnary.org, "Godhead here in hiding," https://hymnary.org/text/godhead_here_in_hiding

Pope Saint John Paul II, General Audience (Nov. 8, 2000), https://www.vatican.va/content/john-paul-ii/en/audiences/2000/documents/hf_jp-ii_aud_20001108.html.

Pope Saint John Paul II, *Ut Unum Sint* (May 25, 1995) at 101, https://www.vatican.va/content/john-paul-ii/en/encyclicals/documents/hf_jp-ii_enc_25051995_ut-unum-sint.html.

References

Kelly, Mark J. "That Moses Thing," Catholic Answers Magazine (Sept 1, 2000), https://www.catholic.com/magazine/print-edition/that-moses-thing.

Knights of Columbus. "A Scriptural Rosary for the Family," available at https://www.kofc.org/en/resources/faith-in-action-programs/faith/rosary-program/319-scriptural-rosary.pdf.

Kosloski, Philip. "What do the Alpha and Omega represent in Christian art?" Aleteia (May 29, 2017), https://aleteia.org/2017/05/29/what-do-the-alpha-and-omega-represent-in-christian-art.

Kosloski, Philip. "St. Bernardine of Siena's prayer to the Holy Name of Jesus," Aleteia (Jan. 14, 2019), https://aleteia.org/2019/01/14/st-bernardine-of-sienas-prayer-to-the-holy-name-of-jesus.

Kunnappally, Ephrem. *Highway to Heaven: A Spiritual Journey through the Life of Blessed Carlo Acutis* (Pavanatma Publishers 2020).

Lori, Most Rev. William E., Archbishop of the Archdiocese of Baltimore. "Eucharist: Sacrament of Unity," *Catholic Review* (June 11, 2021), https://catholicreview.org/eucharist-sacrament-of-unity.

Maere, R. "IHS," The Catholic Encyclopedia, New York: Robert Appleton Company, 1910, https://www.newadvent.org/cathen/07649a.htm

McNamara, Reverend Edward. "Where the Tabernacle Should Be," *Zenit Daily Dispatch* (Jan. 27, 2004), https://www.ewtn.com/catholicism/library/where-the-tabernacle-should-be-4377.

O'Connor, John Cardinal, Pontifical North American College website at https://www.pnac.org/support/prayers-for-seminarians/

Opus Dei, "Meditations: First Sunday of Saint Joseph" (Jan. 29, 2023), https://opusdei.org/en/article/first-sunday-of-saint-joseph/.

"Prayer for Unity: Anonymous Meditation Based on Eucharistic Prayer for Reconciliation II," Diocese of San Angelo website, https://sanangelodiocese.org/prayer-for-unity. Used with permission.

"Prayer to Saint Joseph for the Whole Church," *Catholic.org*, https://www.catholic.org/prayers/prayer.php?p=587.

"Praying the Holy Rosary with Saint Josemaria." Available on Amazon and from the Saint Josemaria Institute at https://stjosemaria.org/product/praying-the-holy-rosary-with-st-josemaria.

"The Golden Arrow," *Our Catholic Prayers*, https://www.ourcatholicprayers.com/golden-arrow.html.

Rottman, Reverend Nicholas. "Born in Bethlehem – the 'House of Bread'" *Source and Summit* (Diocese of Covington Oct. 13, 2020) https://covdio.org/born-in-bethlehem-the-house-of-bread.

Rozell, Lynda. "Angels in Chicago," Tin Can Pilgrim blog (Oct. 9, 2019), https://tincanpilgrim.com/2019/10/09/angels-in-chicago.

Rozell, Lynda. *Journeys with a Tin Can Pilgrim: from corporate lawyer to Airstream nomad* (St. John's Press 2021).

Sacred Heart Catholic Church, "The Tabernacle," https://www.shcbloomfield.org/the-tabernacle.

Saunders, Reverend William. "What Are the Symbols of the Four Evangelists?" *Catholic Exchange* (Aug. 19, 2020), https://catholicexchange.com/what-are-the-symbols-of-the-four-evangelists.

Saunders, Reverend William. "What is the Symbolism of the Pelican Feeding Little Pelicans?" *Catholic Straight Answers*, https://catholicstraightanswers.com/what-is-the-symbolism-of-the-pelican-feeding-little-pelicans.

Schaefer, Reverend Francis. "The Tabernacle: Its History, Structure, and Custody," *The Ecclesiastical Review* Vol. 92, No. 5 (May 1935), https://play.google.com/books/reader?id=-8zNAAAAMAAJ&pg=GBS.PA448-IA4&hl=en.

Schneider, Victoria. *The Bishop of the Abandoned Tabernacle: Saint Manual Gonzalez Garcia* (Scepter Publishers 2018).

Seitz, Reverend Wolfgang. "St. Thérèse and the Priesthood" St. Therese Church, http://www.sttheresechurchalhambra.org/?DivisionID=10357&DepartmentID=25315.

Sullivan, Charles T.. "Four evangelists' symbols came from themes in their Gospels" *Arkansas Catholic* (May 5, 2007), https://www.dolr.org/article/four-evangelists%E2%80%99-symbols-came-themes-their-gospels.

The Divine Mercy, "How to Recite the Chaplet," https://www.thedivinemercy.org/message/devotions/pray-the-chaplet.

Thiron, Rita. "The Roman Missal: The Gloria," *Faith, The Magazine of the Catholic Diocese of Lansing* (May 2011), https://faithmag.com/roman-missal-gloria. See also Luke 2:14.

USCCB, "Basic Prayers: Memorare," https://www.usccb.org/prayers/memorare.

USCCB. "General Instruction of the Roman Missal (2010)," https://www.usccb.org/prayer-and-worship/the-mass/general-instruction-of-the-roman-missal.

USCCB. "How to Pray the Chaplet of Divine Mercy," https://www.usccb.org/prayers/how-pray-chaplet-divine-mercy.

USCCB, "Litany of the Holy Name of Jesus," https://www.usccb.org/prayers/litany-holy-name-jesus.

USCCB. "Rosaries," available at https://www.usccb.org/prayer-and-worship/prayers-and-devotions/rosaries.

USCCB, *The Saint Therese Vocation Society Brochure* (Diocese of Arlington Office of Vocations), https://www.usccb.org/resources/st-terese-vocation-society-adult-english.pdf.

Van den Biesen, Christian. "Alpha and Omega." *The Catholic Encyclopedia*. Vol. 1. New York: Robert Appleton Company, 1907, http://www.newadvent.org/cathen/01332b.htm.

Van Sloun, Reverend Michael. "Different Portrayals of the Holy Spirit as a Dove," *The Catholic Spirit* (June 7, 2019), https://thecatholicspirit.com/commentary/hotdish/different-portrayals-of-the-holy-spirit-as-a-dove.

Van Sloun, Reverend Michael. "Tabernacles Inside and Outside of Church," *The Catholic Spirit* (Nov. 21, 2019), https://thecatholicspirit.com/faith/focus-on-faith/faith-fundamentals/tabernacles-inside-and-outside-of-church.

Van Sloun, Reverend Michael. "Why the Pelican with Chicks Is a Symbol of the Eucharist," *The Catholic Spirit*, (Jan. 23, 2019), https://thecatholicspirit.com/faith/focus-on-faith/faith-fundamentals/why-the-pelican-with-chicks-is-a-symbol-of-the-eucharist.

Vianney Vocations. "Prayer for Vocations before the Blessed Sacrament. https://vianneyvocations.com/product/prayer-card-blessed-sacrament.

Winters, Jaimie Julia. "Tabernacles change through time but have always been where God dwells," *Jersey Catholic* (March 28, 2023), https://jerseycatholic.org/tabernacles-change-through-time-but-have-always-been-where-god-dwells-photos-2.

Word on Fire Institute, "Adoro Te Devote," translated by Gerard Manley Hopkins and read by Jonathan Roumie (June 22, 2022), https://youtu.be/nItzkIJL7JM?si=q-soZPT3zVRxFceu.

Zahorik, Lyn. "Fish symbol has deep roots," *The Compass* (Diocese of Green Bay Wisconsin: Feb. 7, 2013), https://www.thecompassnews.org/2013/02/fish-symbol-has-deep-roots.

Zimmerman, Rabbi Jack. "Sukkot; The Feast of Booths" *Jewish Voice* (Dec. 1, 2015), https://www.jewishvoice.org.

APPENDIX

Photographs by State or Other Location

Unless otherwise specified, all photographs were taken by Lynda Rozell. You'll find them in the chapter and section indicated in parentheses next to the location.

Arizona

- Saint John Neumann Catholic Church, Yuma (Chapter Six: Jesus, Life of Jesus Christ)

Colorado

- Sacred Heart Catholic Church, Colorado Springs (Chapter Five: Sacrifice, The Lamb)
- St. Mary's Cathedral, Colorado Springs (Chapter Six: Jesus, Life of Jesus Christ)

California

- Mission San Antonio de Padua, Jolon (Chapter Six: Jesus, Life of Jesus Christ)
- St. Francis of Assisi Catholic Church, La Quinta (Chapter Six: Jesus, Light of the World)
- American Martyrs Catholic Church, Manhattan Beach (photograph provided by church) (Chapter Four: Nourishment, The Last Supper)

- Mission Basilica San Juan Capistrano, San Juan Capistrano (Chapter Six: Jesus, Life of Jesus Christ)
- Mission San Luis Obispo, San Luis Obispo (Chapter Four: Nourishment, The Blessed Sacrament)
- Mission Soledad Catholic Chapel, Soledad (Chapter Six: Jesus, Anchor)
- St. Francis de Solano Catholic Church, Sonoma (Chapter Six: Jesus, Christograms)
- Mission Basilica San Buenaventura, Ventura (Chapter Six: Jesus, The Good Shepherd)

District of Columbia

- "Chapel of the Blessed Sacrament," Basilica of the National Shrine of the Immaculate Conception, Washington, D.C. Photographer Lynda Rozell. Used with permission of the National Shrine, 2023. (Chapter Three: Where to Find Tabernacles)
- Blessed Sacrament Chapel, Cathedral of St. Matthew the Apostle (Chapter Eight: The Church, The Four Evangelists)

Florida

- Ave Maria Catholic Church, Ave Maria (Chapter Eight: The Church, Cathedrals and Churches)
- St. Peter the Fisherman Catholic Church, Big Pine Key (Chapter Five: Sacrifice, Overview)

Appendix: Photographs by State or Other Location

- Blessed Sacrament Catholic Church, Clermont (Chapter Four: Nourishment, Deer at Fountain)
- St. Patrick Catholic Church, Mt. Dora (Chapter Nine: Mission, Unity)
- Basilica of the Immaculate Conception, Jacksonville (Chapter Three: Where to Find Tabernacles)
- St. Patrick Catholic Church, Miami Beach (photograph by James Dwight Davis © All Rights Reserved. Used with Permission) (Chapter Five: Sacrifice, The Pelican)
- Christ Our Redeemer Catholic Church, Niceville (Chapter Seven: Spirit, Angels)
- St. Maximilian Kolbe Catholic Church, Port Charlotte (Chapter Six: Jesus, Christograms)
- St. Anastasia Catholic Church, Saint Augustine (Chapter Three: Where to Find Tabernacles)
- Mary, Mother of God Chapel, San Pedro Spiritual Development Center, Winter Park (Chapter Four: Nourishment, Grain and Grapes)

Georgia

- Sacred Heart Catholic Church, Milledgeville (Chapter Four: Nourishment, The Blessed Sacrament)

Illinois

- Saint Stanislaus Kosta Catholic Church, Chicago (photograph provided by church) (Chapter Nine: Mission, Living Tabernacles)

- St. Malachy Catholic Church, Rantoul (Chapter Six: Jesus, Anchor)

Indiana

- St. Joan of Arc Catholic Church, Indianapolis (Chapter Two: History and Development of the Tabernacle)

Maine

- St. Anne's Catholic Church, Gorham (Chapter Five: Sacrifice, The Pelican)
- Cathedral of the Immaculate Conception Chapel, Portland (Chapter Eight: The Church, Cathedrals and Churches)
- Our Lady of Perpetual Help, Windham (Chapter Six: Jesus, Light of the World)
- St. Philip Catholic Church, Auburn (Chapter Four: Nourishment, The Blessed Sacrament)

Maryland

- Eucharistic Dove, French early 13th century, courtesy of The Walters Art Museum, Baltimore, MD. Creative Common License CC0 (Chapter Two: History and Development of the Tabernacle)
- St. Anthony's Catholic Church, North Beach (Chapter Nine: Mission, Fish)

Appendix: Photographs by State or Other Location 187

Massachusetts

- Blessed Sacrament Chapel, Cathedral of the Holy Cross, Boston (Chapter Eight: The Church, The Four Evangelists)
- Bethany Chapel, Archdiocese of Boston Pastoral Center, Braintree (Chapter Seven: Spirit, The Holy Spirit)
- St. Oscar Romero Parish, Canton (Chapter Nine: Mission, Unity)
- Arnold Hall Conference Center Chapel, Pembroke (Chapter Six: Jesus, Life of Jesus Christ)

Michigan

- Sacred Heart Catholic Church, Caro (Chapter Six: Jesus, Life of Jesus Christ)
- Blessed Trinity Catholic Church, Frankenmuth (Chapter Nine: Mission, Fish)
- Our Lady of Good Counsel, Plymouth (Chapter Nine: Mission, Living Tabernacles)
- St. Francis Xavier Cabrini Catholic Church, Vassar (Chapter Four: Nourishment, Overview)

Mississippi

- Nativity of the Blessed Virgin Mary Cathedral, Biloxi (Chapter Six: Jesus, Christograms)

Missouri

- St. James Catholic Church, Potosi (Chapter Two: History and Development of the Tabernacle)

Nebraska

- St. Luke Catholic Church, Ogallala (Chapter Six: Jesus, Light of the World)

New Jersey

- Sacred Heart Catholic Church, Bloomfield (photographs provided by church) (Chapter Nine: Mission, Fish)
- Our Lady of the Lake, Mount Arlington (Chapter Four: Nourishment, Overview)
- Resurrection Roman Catholic Church, Randolph (Chapter Seven: Spirit, The Holy Spirit)
- Shrine of St. Joseph, Stirling (Chapter Seven: Spirit, The Holy Spirit)

New Mexico

- St. Joseph on the Rio Grande, Albuquerque (Chapter Five: Sacrifice, Overview)

Appendix: Photographs by State or Other Location

New York

- St. Frances Xavier Cabrini Shrine, New York City (Chapter Four: Nourishment, Grain and Grapes)
- Riverside Study Center Oratory, New York City (photograph by Brian Finnerty, Opus Dei Communications Office) (Chapter Eight: The Church, Cathedrals and Churches)
- St. Thomas Catholic Church, Staten Island (Chapter Four: Nourishment, Loaves and Fishes) (Chapter Nine: Mission, Unity)

North Dakota

- St. Bernard's Catholic Church, Belfield (Chapter Two: History and Development of the Tabernacle)

Ohio

- St. Paul Catholic Church, Englewood (Chapter Five: Sacrifice, The Lamb)

Tennessee

- St. Philip Catholic Church, Franklin (Chapter Six: Jesus, Light of the World)
- St. Mary's Catholic Church, Jackson (Chapter Eight: The Church, Cathedrals and Churches)

Virginia

- St. Mary of the Immaculate Conception, Fredericksburg (Chapter Eight: The Church, The Four Evangelists) (Chapter Nine: Mission, Living Tabernacles)

Washington

- St. Charles Borromeo Catholic Church, Tacoma (Chapter Four: Nourishment, Overview)

West Virginia

- St. James the Greater Catholic Church, Charles Town (Chapter Eight: The Church, Cathedrals and Churches)

Wyoming

- St. Patrick Catholic Church, Casper (Chapter Five: Sacrifice, The Lamb)
- Wyoming Catholic College Chapel, Lander (Chapter Six: Jesus, Christograms)
- Our Lady of Sorrows Catholic Church, Rock Springs (Chapter Four: Nourishment, Grain and Grapes)

Mid-Atlantic State

- Unspecified Catholic Church, Mid-Atlantic State (anonymity at request of pastor) (Chapter Seven: Spirit, Angels)

Israel

- Model of Old Testament Tabernacle, Timna Park, Israel. Creative Commons Attribution - ShareAlike 4.0 International, https://commons.wikimedia.org/wiki/user.Mboesch (Chapter Two: History and Development of the Tabernacle)

Made in the USA
Middletown, DE
15 February 2025